MW01493369

4WD TRAILS & GHOST TOWNS OF COLORADO

PASS PATROL RECOLLECTIONS V-1

by

Larry E Heck

DISCLAIMER

This book is an accumulation of stories that appeared in publications written by Larry E Heck including Volume One of the Adventures of Pass Patrol. Each story is from a time and place where members of Pass Patrol traveled together or separately. Character names were those chosen by individuals as their club handles. Any resemblance or similarity to names, people or facts involving non-members that currently exist or existed in the past are purely coincidental. Many of the stories in this book are simply campfire tales told and retold around campfires with the intention of be humorous and not necessarily accurate.

Contents

INTRODUCTION

I moved to Colorado in September of 1984, transferred from Michigan. I was a district manager in the Customer Service Division and had already been with Datapoint Corporation for eight years Previous promotions with transfers included Wichita, KS, St. Louis, MO, Pittsburgh, PA and Detroit, MI.

Prior to my latest transfer to Denver, the marketing division of the company made serious errors in its revenue reporting. The stock value of the company plummeted overnight making it ripe fruit for a hostile takeover by a corporate raider. He split the company into two parts. The customer service division was renamed Intelogic Trace (IT) with the intention of draining it dry and closing it down. Because the customer service division was so profitable, it took him another seven years to get it done.

While he was doing whatever corporate raiders do, I continued to run the Denver District on the profitable side of the scale. On the other hand, I had developed a keen interest in those mountains I looked at every day on the way to work. I needed time away from the corporate jungle and those mountains provided a good place to hide.

In August of 1985, I created a tiny 4x4 club named the IT Patrol. It consisted entirely of employees from my district that had an interest in exploring the Rocky Mountains. Our first of two trips in 1985 took us across some of the state's highest mountain passes. I loved every second of it. I wrote about those first two trips and made the stories available to everyone in my district.

I have always been a writer. I was born with it and considered it to be a curse. I never wanted to be a writer, but every time I paused to see what I was doing, I had written something else. At the age of about five or six I was putting the words I learned at school to paper. Relatives that visited the farm house would search for stories I might have left lying around. They were stories from the mind of a child that adults found amusing.

Prior to being transferred to Denver, I was doing a lot of writing. Some on paper and some on computers. During the time I was District Manager in Pittsburgh, I needed accurate and timely reports for service calls from the previous day to see how much was left over when I came to work in the morning. There was nothing in the corporation that could do that for me, so I wrote a computer program called FRS (Field Reporting System). It was my creation, but when upper management saw what it could do, I was tasked with implementing it nationwide. I was transferred to the regional office in Detroit to make that happen. To complete the project involved nine months of writing, revising, and rewriting day after day to make the program compatible with every district and regional office in the country.

Weekly newsletters were always my favorites during the times I was in district manager positions. They were written to keep my employees informed and focused on our challenges and how we could meet and exceed company goals. In Denver, the weekly reports continued, so I was frequently writing. Taking that writing one step further by writing for the public was a natural progression.

As already mentioned, I wrote about those first trips to the mountains in 1985. At first, it was called the IT Report and only available to those in my district. Many who read it suggested I put it up for sale to the public. In 1986, I renamed it and advertised in coupon clippers published in the local newspaper. Surprisingly, people bought it.

I renamed my club to give it a more public appeal. Initially, there were only about a dozen of us in what became known as the Pass Patrol 4x4 Travel Club. Using those same coupon clippers, I began selling memberships to the public. Each trip was a new adventure. There were the places I had been to before and those I had only heard of. A popular term became, "Boldly going where we had never gone before."

At the end of the 1986, I wrote my first guide book but had no luck finding a publisher. A manager I once worked for, told a group in a meeting that I was not one to be stopped by obstacles. To me they were opportunities. He told them I would get to my objective by going around, over, or through any obstacle in my way. Rejections from publishers created an obstacle that could not stand.

In 1987, I purchased a used printing press from a company that had upgraded. The owner of the company spent several days teaching me how to use it. I published the first in a series called the Adventures of Pass Patrol. "4WD Trails and Ghost Towns of Colorado." It has gone through many revisions, but the original stories remained the same. Before I could get the books into book stores, it needed to be more than fifty pages. Additional stories were added making the book 100 pages long. This book is a collection of the stories that were in it.

By the time my books were available in bookstores and gift shops throughout Colorado, there were four volumes in the series. A two-hour video of each volume was also available. The Adventures of Pass eventually expanded to seven volumes. Although I ended that series in 1999, those products were available for many more years. Used copies can still be found in some markets.

I continued writing for a national magazine until 2013. There are many volumes of material from those days that could also become books but for now they are only available at the magazine web site.

I sold the rights to publish the Adventures of Pass Patrol in 2006. The people I sold it to were not successful and the business folded. Fortunately, I only sold the rights to that one series. I retained the right to republish everything in that series under a different name.

That was then. This is now. Welcome to "Pass Patrol Recollections." Volume One.

Pass Patrol Recollections is an attempt to give life back to stories that are fading into history. Some will say the stories from that time were tales, and often referred to as fictional. No doubt they were embellished. The term we used around the campfire was. "Every story we tell has a spark of truth in it somewhere."

They were intended to be entertaining and not entirely factual. The only fact was that each time they were told around the campfire, they changed a little. The stories included here are much the same as when they were first published.

Be aware that many photos used in the original publication are no longer available. In those days, there were no digital cameras within the budget of a lowly freelance writer. You will find that many photos are different than in the original guide books. That means you will see vehicles pictured that were not yet built in 1986. Although they may be different they are still on the trail being featured.

Navigation in Pass Patrol Recollections is different from the first book. In those days, GPS units were very inaccurate. By referencing Google Maps, Topo USA, and other software, we have attempted to reconstruct the navigation charts. Even for the stories that did not previously have GPS.

Odometer/trip meter readings can vary a lot from yours. We used a variety of vehicles in getting these figures. Tire sizes and level of tire inflation caused them to all read differently. Use the odometer readings as a reference but do not rely on them entirely.

FREELANCE WRITER

Larry E Heck

CB Handle: Outlaw

Founder

Author

Pass Patrol Recollections

It came alive in '85,
Its wheels began to roll,
As a group of friends, women and men,
formed the Pass Patrol.

With weekend supplies and 4-wheel drives,
they seek forgotten trails.
To explore the past and help it last
and uncover ghost town tales.

They bounce and bump, over boulders and stumps
and tread water up to the door;
They use 4-wheel low, through mud and snow,
in search of tales and lore.

Across rivers and creeks, and snow-covered peaks;
through canyons with mile-high walls;
past deserted mines, through Rocky Mountain pines,
past tumbling clear water falls,

They slip and slide, across the divide,
it's 4-wheelers on the roll.
If your life's a bore, there's gotta be more:
Join the Pass Patrol!

OUTLAW'S CODE

Everywhere we go, with everything we do, every time we look around, someone is calling us, outlaws. There are those who spend long hours dedicated to the purpose of keeping our misguided image alive. They send camera crews to tape vandals driving off established trails and tell viewers those vandals are 4-wheelers. "4-wheelers are outlaws!"

Isn't it amazing how easy it is to grow our outlaw image? Even the manufacturers of the vehicles we drive feed it. In an effort to promote the capabilities of their vehicles, they show us ripping across virgin country at 60 miles per hour. Our enemies say, "4-wheelers are outlaws!"

I once saw a vehicle ad in a magazine showing a 4X4 driving on the wrong side of a guard rail along a paved highway. Our enemies pointed at it and said, "4-wheelers are outlaws!"

WARNING!

Many of the roads in this book are in danger of being closed by future Wilderness Bills and management plans. When a Wilderness Bill is passed or a management plan is implemented, roads within its boundaries are closed forever. Such actions lock out the handicapped and physically impaired. We will never see those public lands again! Our lands!

NEVER!

I have been 4-wheeling since long before it was called 4-wheeling. When I was a boy, we called it farming. In all those years, I have never seen a 4-wheeler rip across virgin country at 60 miles per hour or drive on the wrong side of a guard rail. We are usually the ones going, "Putt, Putt" along some dusty secluded trail at a pace slightly faster than a tired jogger, or winching through a rutted-out section of the trail while wishing we had locked in the hubs before entering it. "Are we outlaws?"

There is something romantic ... mysterious ... even admirable about being an outlaw ... about living by an Outlaw Code of Honor. The 4-wheeler code of honor is, "Tread Lightly". We live it by staying on existing roads. We earn the notches on our guns by tackling the toughest roads our expertise will allow. We can rustle up support for our code by insisting advertisers display it in their ads.

Nearly 100 years ago, there were three notorious outlaw hide-outs. "Hole in The Wall", "Robbers Roost", and "Brown's Hole". They were the home of the Outlaws and they were kept safe by the Outlaw Code. That code kept peace within and kept the law out. Eventually, the code weakened, the outlaws were disbanded, and the law moved in, shutting down all three hide-outs.

Today, our hide-outs are the public lands. Some individuals, wearing the badge of the law, are moving in to shut them down with Wilderness Bills, BLM Management Plans, or National Forest Management Plans. They portray us as outlaws because everyone knows outlaws must be kept out.

The only way to shoot it out with them is with a law of our own ... a code ... the Outlaw Code, (Tread Lightly). If we are going to keep our hide-outs, we must demonstrate that 4-wheelers are not the vandals who drive off trails. We must get that message to our senators, the National Forest Service, the Bureau of Land Management, and to the manufacturers of the products we use. Maybe it's time we started a new beginning ... the beginning of a new image for us ... Outlaws?

RED CONE

The most dangerous trail in the state?

Many years ago, my brother (CB handle - Santa Anna) came out to visit me for the first time. We were sitting on the back porch of my house out in Aurora and admiring the mountains on the other side of Denver's brown cloud.

"That's mighty pretty," Santa Anna commented. "It sure would be nice if a fella could go sit on one of those peaks for a while."

"You wanna do it now?" I asked.

Two hours later, I pulled onto County Road 60 just west of Grant with my brother and his wife both in the truck. It was their first time 4-wheeling so they had never seen such beautiful scenery before. At the end of County Road 60, the trail forks in three directions. The one on the left is a dead end. The one in the middle goes to Webster Pass. It's a nasty trail with very narrow ledges, and is normally blocked by snow until August. The trail on the right goes to Webster Pass too, but it does so by going over the 12,801-foot peak of a mountain called Red Cone.

Red Cone attracts 4-wheelers like girls attract boys. No matter what you do, you can't keep'um away ... and when you ask'um why ... all they do is giggle.

Red Cone has appeared in magazines many times. It's been praised as the "HILL THAT WILL THRILL YOU!" and it's been cursed as the "HILL THAT WILL KILL YOU!" We don't know of anyone who died on Red Cone but some have rolled over.

In the photo below, Pass Patrol tackled Red Cone on a sunny day.

Getting to the peak of Red Cone is serious 4-wheeling for a stock vehicle but not really dangerous unless the driver makes a serious mistake. Going down the other side is the one that separates the sane from the not-so-sane. Sane folks will turn around and go back the way they came in. But the rest of us ... those who make a habit out of living on the edge ... just gotta go down the other side.

The first time I questioned another 4-wheeler about what Red Cone was like, he said, "It's easy. All ya gotta do is ease the bumper over the edge ... and hang on."

If you've never driven off a cliff before, Red Cone will be a new experience for you. It is so steep, you can't see what the surface looks like while standing on the peak of the mountain. To appreciate the Montezuma side of Red Cone, you must be there.

The three of us were standing on that peak and looking over the edge.

"That ain't no road," Nancy said. She looked at the grin on my face and then back at Santa Anna. "If you're gonna drive down that, I'll walk down ahead of you and get some pictures."

"I advise against doing that," I responded. "Red Cone is too steep to walk down. You'll slip on the pebbles and fall."

My advice was too late. Nancy was already going downhill with her camcorder on her shoulder. We watched as she disappeared over the edge, then we heard a short scream followed by some foreign language I never heard before.

"I didn't know Nancy could speak a foreign language," I remarked.

"She can't," Santa Anna chuckled. "We better go down and get her."

We climbed into the truck, shifted into low-low, set the emergency brake at four clicks, and idled carefully down the slope. The trick to conquering Red Cone, is to keep the wheels from locking up. If they do, the back end of the vehicle will begin sliding around. If the vehicle gets sideways on Red Cone, IT WILL ROLL OVER. There are 4-wheelers living in the good ole USA who proved it.

The one thing you don't want to happen is for the back end of the vehicle to catch up with the front end. Slamming on the brakes can cause that to happen. On the other hand, giving her more gas (not too much - just a shot) will cause her to straighten out slicker than a garden snake between two Dobermans. Hang on tight though. The rest of the ride will be a buckaroo bonsai adventure.

The picture below includes the Webster Pass Trail coming up from the left. It is still covered in snow.

GETTING TO RED CONE

You can find Grant, Co. on Highway 285 west of Denver,

About three miles west of grant is a road on the right with signs designating it as county road 60.

Go past the Halls Valley Campground and you will find a three-way intersection.

Webster Pass is easy, but very narrow and leans toward the cliff edge. The snow drift at the top does not melt in some years.

Red Cone ... is ... Red Cone.

GETTING LOST IN STYLE

The Gunnison National Forest Map covers the area. The USGS maps of the area are Gunnison County #3 and Pitkin County #2.

THINK ABOUT IT

Before you decide to take this hill, think about what you have on your side. The first thing everyone thinks about is their brakes. Consider, if your master cylinder fails, you won't have any brakes. A master cylinder is not a mechanical link. It uses fluid pressure to operate. One blown seal and you have no more pressure.

So, what if you are going down Red Cone and your master cylinder pops its cork. What's left?

Emergency brake comes to mind. It is a mechanical link, but most emergency brakes are designed to keep a vehicle from moving when it's stopped ... not to stop it when it's moving. When we leave the top of Red Cone, we normally set the emergency brake just enough to drag but not enough to lock up.

The only thing left after that is engine drag. If you have a manual transmission, you have a mechanical link between the engine and the wheels. That won't stop the vehicle, but it will slow it down in direct proportion to the gear ratio and engine back pressure.

If you have an automatic transmission, you have hydraulic pumps that are designed to slip. Unless that tranny has been modified, it probably won't be much help.

In other words, after all the add'n & subtract'n is done, losing a master cylinder on Red Cone could be a good plot for the next, "Fatal Attraction".

If it does happen, remember to keep your cool so you won't embarrass yourself. Take off your hat, wave it in a tight circle like a bull rider, and holler, "Yeee Hawww!"

I drive Red Cone nearly every year. In all those trips, I have never lost a master cylinder, never had a close call, and never gone sideways on the hill. In fact, the only time I ever hurt myself on Red Cone was when I walked down to take pictures of other 4-wheelers. That's how I knew Nancy was gonna bust her whatsit.

By the time we reached Nancy, she was almost at the bottom, camcorder running, with her ego and some other parts slightly bruised. She had plenty to say but the bottom line was, "It's real pretty, but when we come back I ain't gonna walk down. It's too dangerous!

RED CONE NAVIGATION

The following odometer readings were taken using a '97 Isuzu Trooper. The GPS positions were acquired by referencing Google Maps.

ODO	Latitude N	Longitude W	Landmarks and descriptions
0.0	39.456698	105.721446	Travel west of Grant on Highway 285 turn onto County Road 60.
5.0	39.483099	105.804262	Go right at the intersection past the Hand Cart Campground.
Then immediately turn right on 565. Turn right again on the first trail for Red Cone.			
10.5	39.527003	105.822037	This is the peak of Red Cone Mountain. 12,801 feet.
11.2	39.531247	105.832452	Webster Pass. Right goes to Montezuma
12.6	39.537579	105.841245	Stay right for Montezuma. Left is Radical Hill

RED CONE MAP

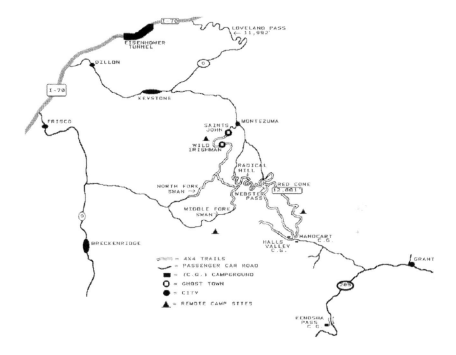

The End for Red Cone

HAPPY TRAILS!

MOUNT BROSS

Park on the peak of a Colorado Fourteener – 14,169 ft.

NOTE: Much of the land on Mt. Bross is on private land and may be posted. The road may be closed by land owners. Check with the BLM office in Fairplay for maps.

Having grown up in Illinois, I realize most people east of the Kansas border think the only mountain worth anything in Colorado is Pike's Peak.

The old cabin at Windy Ridge is falling down.

That's all we heard about in school and it was plastered on calendars in nearly every store. What a disappointment I felt the first time I went to the top of Pike's Peak. Sure, it was pretty, but so commercialized.

When my relatives come out to visit, I always take them to Pike's Peak first because they won't be able to face the folks back home if they don't have at least one picture of the family standing in front of the Pike's Peak sign at the summit. Once all that tourist stuff is out of the way, I ask, "Are you ready to go to one of the big ones now?"

"Big one," they ask. "You mean Pike is not the biggest one of all?"

"Naw! Pike is just a baby. It's only 14,110 ft. tall standing on its tippy toes. Now … Mt. Bross … That's a real mountain, 59 feet taller, nestled right in the middle of other fourteeners, with a view of mountain tops in every direction."

There is no doubt in my mind. Mt. Bross is the best mountain within a day's drive of Denver to take a flatlander on his first trip to the Rocky Mountains. If he or she just loves Mt. Bross, try one of the rough ones, like Mt. Antero. In other words, break them in slowly.

Mt. Bross is no challenge for any 4X4 with a low range, but it will frighten those who don't like shelf roads or heights.

Its peak is flat, large enough to hold a football stadium, with room left to park, and it can be driven from end to end and side to side. The view in all directions includes lakes, mountains, and valleys.

The wind blows most of the time and is normally nippy on the hottest summer day. An easy hiking path crosses a hogback to Mt. Lincoln, but flatlanders should not be hiking at these altitudes. To the west, 2,000 feet straight down, is Kite Lake and campground where hikers park their motor homes and begin the very strenuous trek to the peak.

Along the way to the peak, remains of old mining camps add to the enjoyment of the trip. Windy Ridge is tucked away in some trees and marks the official beginning of the 4X4 trail. Much of this area is on private land and the road is likely to be closed someday. Check with the BLM office in Fairplay.

Other shacks are scattered along the mountainside high above tree line. The most interesting for us is the bunk house, complete with bunks. During much of the year, these structures are filled with snow.

MT BROSS NAVIGATION

The following odometer readings were taken using a '97 Isuzu Trooper. The GPS positions were acquired by referencing Google Maps.

ODO	Latitude N	Longitude W	Landmarks and descriptions
0.0	39.283820	106.062728	Begin in Alma, Colorado.
Turn west on the road for Kite Lake. It should be marked as County Road 8. Reset your trip meter.			
2.7			Follow the creek on CR8 to FSR415 and turn right.
11.1	39.336468	106.108409	Go to the top of the pass between Mt. Lincoln and Mt. Bross.
At that point, the trail splits. Going straight goes partly down the other side and turning right goes to Mt. Lincoln. Turn hard left and drive on up to the very top of the mountain. That last section is a little tricky, but not too difficult.			
	39.335206	106.107652	Top of Mt. Bross.

MT. BROSS AND THE GENERAL AREA MAP

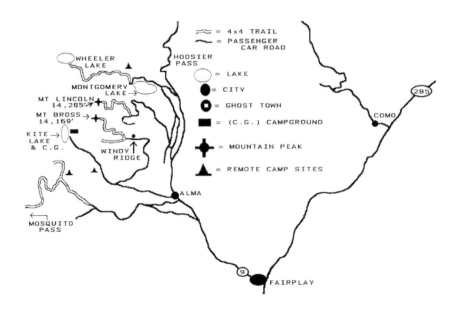

The End for Mt Bross.

HAPPY TRAILS!

MOUNT LINCOLN

14,284 feet in elevation

NOTE: Much of the land on Mt. Lincoln is on private land and may be posted. At the time of this writing, the road was open although signs on both sides of the road deliver a confusing message. Check with the BLM office in Fairplay for maps.

At 14,284 feet above the sea, Mt. Lincoln is one of Colorado's highest points. The area around the mountain was the center of history-in-the-making during the 1860s. Most of that activity involved our state's version of Atlantis ... a very wet ghost town named Montgomery. If you have your scuba gear, you might look for it at the bottom of the reservoir pictured below.

We call it Atlantis because its only inhabitants are fish. It sits at the bottom of Montgomery Reservoir in the same spot where it was in 1861. That was the year it was proposed as the new state capitol. Imagining such a town as rivaling Denver in population is not easy, but during the year of 1861, the two cities were very similar in size. The difference was a matter of destiny. Montgomery was a boom town and such towns vanished as quickly as they materialized. A few years after being proposed as the state capitol, it was nothing but empty shacks.

During Montgomery's boom, Mt. Lincoln was named. Citizens of mining camps often passed the time by thinking up names for mountains ... but this one was special. They named it after President Lincoln and sealed it by sending him a bar of pure gold.

President Lincoln was delighted with his gift and sent Schuyler Colfax, a member of his cabinet, to Montgomery to express his gratitude. (If anyone wants to send a bar of gold to me, I'll deliver my thanks in person.)

According to local lore, Colfax took his fiancée on a hike to the top of Mt. Lincoln where she accepted his proposal to be married. One old timer jokingly added, "She'd promised anything as long as he got her off that mountain 'fore dark." Even on the hottest summer day, Mt. Lincoln's night-time wind and temperature can be brutal.

The trail up the side of Mt. Lincoln is an easy one most of the way. There are a few switchbacks near the top to get one's attention, but nothing in comparison to many others in the state. Near the trail's end, there are spur trails going in various directions, but none of them go all the way to the peak so any one is as good as the other.

Mt. Lincoln is a good trail for beginners. It is wide and relatively smooth. Just don't drive too close to the edge.

NAVIGATION FOR MT LINCOLN

**The following odometer readings were taken using a '97 Isuzu Trooper.
The GPS positions were acquired by referencing Google Maps.**

ODO	Latitude N	Longitude W	Landmarks and descriptions
0.0	39.290218	106.066779	Start from Alma, Colorado.
Go north on route 9 to the city limits sign and reset your trip meter to zero.			
1.5	39.312402	106.059483	Turn left on Park County 4.
3.2	39.339255	106.058863	Turn left and cross the creek.
3.5	39.339032	106.062760	Turn right on Roberts Road. Follow switchbacks on the gravel road.
5.2	39.339143	106.075607	Turn right on Forest Service Road 437. You are on the way.

GETTING LOST IN STYLE

The Pike National Forest Service Map includes this entire area. The USGS County Maps have more detail. Mt. Bross, Mt. Lincoln, and Wheeler Lake are in Park County.

MT. LINCOLN MAP AND THE GENERAL AREA.

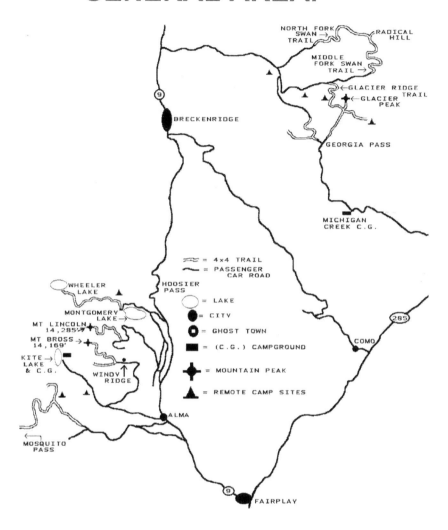

The End for Mt Lincoln.

Happy Trails

WHEELER LAKE

A VDL trail that will test your skill.

This particular trail is one we do every year. Sometimes several times a year. But I'll never do it when it's wet. It's fun enough for me when it's dry.

"Aw come on, Outlaw," Caveman teased. "It can't be that bad. The snow is only a few inches deep."

"You go ahead. I've gotta count the hairs on my head today."

"That won't take long."

"Sure, it will. I'm using my high school graduation picture."

It was right after the first snow in late 1991. The trail was all white and very pretty. Caveman, Texan, and the Man with No Name, had cabin fever so bad they were ready to take on anything so that's exactly what they did. Caveman was having trouble getting his Jimmy through one of the tough spots so he decided to get out and have a closer look.

The door on his Jimmy was open and the emergency brake decided not to hold. That's when the trail began living up to its VDL rating. As the truck rolled backward, a big rock grabbed onto that door and just refused to let go. By the time the Jimmy came to a stop the door didn't look like a door anymore and the truck was hung up.

Texan giggled. "Oh well, a screw here and a bolt there. It'll be good as new."

While Caveman and Texan were deciding what to do next, Cavewoman dropped the Jimmy in gear and shoved the gas pedal to the floor using language I don't care to repeat. Snow and slush flew everywhere, then the Jimmy's tires found a grip and that big truck lunged forward, bounced off a tree, and came to a stop right where it was supposed to have been the first time.

Caveman chuckled. "I guess it takes a woman's touch."

No Name was a new guy that hadn't decided on a handle yet so we just called him, No Name. He was really getting a lesson.

"Man! I ain't never seen nothing like that before! Ye Haw!" It was his first time with a Pass Patrol Squad and the first time he had ever been on a VDL trail in his life.

The Pass Patrol definition for VDL is "Vehicle Damage Likely."

"Let's go find another bad spot," he said eagerly. He found one and lost a shock mount getting through. By that time, Caveman's Jimmy was hung up on another rock. It was a great cure for cabin fever. When we finally got all the trucks back home, we were ready to be couch potatoes again.

The trail to Wheeler Lake begins at the West end of Montgomery Reservoir and takes about an hour under ideal conditions. It is   4-wheeling all the way.

Most stock vehicles don't have enough clearance and commit rock abuse the entire distance. If you're looking for a place to break in your skid plates, the Wheeler Lake Trail will get the job done for you.

Several sections of the trail follow the same path as the creek. We've had some time-consuming arguments over whether "The creek follows the trail" or the "Trail follows the creek." Either way, the water can be very deep in the spring. Hidden below the water are huge rocks and deep pockets patiently waiting for the opportunity to eat your vehicle. If the rocks don't get you, the brush will. We call it Colorado pin-striping.

Wheeler Lake is nestled in its mother's arms. Its mother being Wheeler Mountain. The closer we get to it, the more we feel drawn to it. But then 4-wheelers are easily lured by Mother Nature.

The lake is nearly 12,000 feet above the sea and well above tree line. It is deep enough to have fish in it and I am told they do make a great campfire meal. A waterfall feeds the lake and I have still not climbed to the top of it. I think there was a song about that some time back. One of the lines in it was, "One-uh these days, I'm gonna climb that mountain."

Nearby, on the west side of the lake, is an old mine. I haven't been to the back of it yet either. It would probably cave-in on me anyway.

My, My. So many things to do … so little time!

GETTING TO WHEELER LAKE

Go South from Breckenridge on Highway 9. After you go over Hoosier Pass, begin watching for a heavily used gravel road switchback to your right. Follow it to the west end of Montgomery Reservoir. Take a right turn at the intersection and lock your hubs. You will go under an old Ore Chute and past a small campsite on the right. After that, you are on your own.

GETTING LOST IN STYLE

The Pike National Forest Service Map includes this entire area. The USGS County Maps have more detail. Mt. Bross, Mt. Lincoln and Wheeler Lake are all in Park County.

WHEELER LAKE MAP

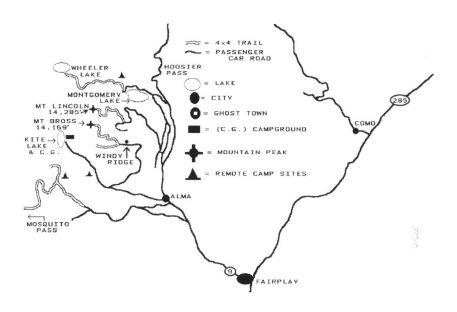

GEORGIA PASS RESCUE

Rescue on Georgia Pass.

"I'll take the Blazer down the mountain," Outlaw announced over the radio. "We'll have to daisy-chain the vehicles from top to bottom."

There was no such thing as "driving" down the ice-packed north slope of Georgia Pass on that day. All Outlaw could do was stand on the brakes and let the Blazer's anti-lock system steer down the trail. Outlaw's passenger seemed a little worried and he had good reason to be. His '94 4Runner had been at the bottom of the hill for three days. The towing companies he called told him they would be happy to go after it next spring. A 4X4 retrieval company had taken one look at it and told him they couldn't save it. Then someone told him there was a crazy outlaw that ran an outfit called Pass Patrol.

A few phone calls later and he was sliding down the mountain in a '95 Blazer with four other winch equipped vehicles waiting for instructions at the top of the pass.

The plan was simple. Outlaw would use his Warn 8000 to pull the 4-Runner to his position. Sundance would use his Warn 12,000 to pull both of them to his position. Wild Coyote would pull the three of them (one at a time of course) using his Warn 9,000 to within reach of Blue Moon's Warn 12,000 and Programmer's Warn 9,000. The plan worked quite well, but took from 2 p.m. until 7 p.m. to complete. In the process, they also rescued a Jeep Cherokee and a Landcruiser that were stuck in the ice.

"I love it when a plan comes together!"

GEORGIA PASS

In Search of Georgia Pass.

"Ain't no way you're gonna get that Rocky over Georgia Pass," he said with a grin.

Seems like there's always somebody who knows a trail nobody else can do. Those challenges normally occur around a campfire when we're swapping lies about all those times we nearly got killed ... or worse.

"No siree. No way at all." He paused to toss another log on the fire. "That there's the roughest trail in the county. Last time I went over it, I busted the hub outta my jeep."

A few weeks later, my son and I (Dusty and Outlaw) took a few days off and went looking for Georgia Pass. We found it too.

Unfortunately, the person who told us about it had never been on it. He was actually on the Glacier Ridge Trail which does begin near Georgia Pass, but we drove around in circles for nearly an entire day before we figured out which was what.

The Georgia Pass trail is a real pussy cat. Except for needing the lower range gears to control our speed in a few places, we had no real need for four-wheel drive.

Our search for Georgia Pass began in Jefferson, Colorado. The road from that side is best described as a graded car road. We pulled up to the Georgia Pass sign and parked next to a Pontiac.

Georgia Pass began as an Indian Trail. War parties tried desperately to maintain exclusive use of the area, and did a pretty good job of keeping the Pale Face away ... until one of'um slipped in and found gold in the Middle Fork Swan Creek. Almost instantly, the valley was packed with people ready to die for the chance to find gold. A fairly large town by the name of Swandyke was erected and mining tunnels were everywhere.

Supply wagons began traveling back and forth between Swandyke and Jefferson. Stagecoaches carried passengers and mail while prospectors traveled back and forth in a steady stream. The Indians moved on.

"Hey, Outlaw." Dusty called. "When is this gonna get rough?"

"Your guess is as good as mine," I answered.

We started down the Breckenridge side of the pass, expecting the worse to meet us head on. We eased along the trail through a beautiful forest, and found lots of rocks to dodge and a few creeks to splash across. We went through one rocky section that required high clearance and then came upon a Buick.

"There ain't no way that Buick came down from the pass so it must have come up from Breckenridge," Dusty commented over the CB " That means this trail is not going to get rough."

"You got that right. That jeep didn't break a hub on this trail."

We followed the trail to the Middle Fork Swan Creek, then turned around and drove back to Georgia Pass. That's where we found the sign, "Glacier Ridge".

NAVIGATION FOR GEORGIA PASS

The following odometer readings were taken using a '97 Isuzu Trooper.
The GPS positions were acquired by referencing Google Maps.

ODO	Latitude N	Longitude W	Landmarks and descriptions
0.0	39.377516	105.800501	Begin in the town of Jefferson. Reset trip meter and turn north on Michigan Creek Road.
5.9	39.411680	105.884508	Follow signs to Michigan creek Campground.
This is a pay campground maintained by the Forest Service.			
11.9	39.458054	105.916595	This is Georgia Pass.
The road to this point is graded for passenger cars. Take the left fork at the sign. Begin descending the slope and enter the forest.			
16.2	39.495096	105.947387	Cross the Middle Fork Swan.
Left goes to Breckenridge. Turn right and have some fun. There are old mining camps to explore.			
18.1			Left. There are campsites on both sides of the creek on the right.
19.5			This is where the Glacier Ridge trail comes out.
If you want to see what the "nasty" section of Glacier Ridge looks like, it's only a 10-minute hike from the intersection. Go across the creek and go right at the next intersection. It's uphill so be ready to huff and puff.			

GLACIER RIDGE

AKA: AXLE CRUSHER

We were back on the summit of Georgia Pass, still wondering where the "nasty" trail was. Our round trip to the Middle Fork Swan over the Georgia Pass Trail had been nothing more than a pleasant cruise through the forest. The USGS map did not show any trails in the area.

We were "Boldly going where we had never gone before!"

A small sign was perched at the top of a post beside an innocent looking trail that spurred off Georgia Pass and disappeared into some trees. Since we never heard of the Glacier Ridge Trail, the sign meant nothing to us.

We assumed the trail was a dead-end campsite. On the other hand, the trail was there so leaving it unexplored never crossed our minds.

Once we made it through the trees, we realized there was more to Glacier Ridge than a quick turn-a-round. The trail split and branched off in three directions.

The trail on the right dead-ended at a campsite. The one in the middle led to the peak of Glacier Peak, 12,853 feet high, but that trail has since been closed. Before inconsiderate government employees closed the trail, it went to one of those Colorado high places where you can stand with one foot on each side of the Continental Divide.

"Breaker 13 for Pass Patrol. How 'bout it Outlaw. You gotta copy on Caveman?"

"Hello Caveman," I responded with surprise. "Where you at?"

"I don't know. We been lost for hours. Where you at?"

"Sitting on top of Glacier Peak."

"We're on the peak of something else," he giggled. "And we got mountains all around us." He paused. "We came up from Montezuma and over Glacier Mountain. We're following a trail that looks like it's headed for the ski slopes of Breckenridge."

Caveman, Engineer, Texin, and Friends were on the trail for North Fork Swan. Using x21 binoculars, we could identify their vehicles on a ridge about four miles north of us.

"Just stay on that trail, Caveman. It'll take you to the Middle Fork Swan in French Gulch. We'll meet you there."

Dusty and I turned north. We still did not know if the trail went all the way through or if it was even the one we were looking for. To add to the excitement, our subconscious minds kept remembering the dare that brought us to Glacier Ridge. "Ain't no way you're gonna get that Rocky ...." Dusty wondered if that went for Broncos too.

From the intersection, the trail we took was just two tire paths skirting the side of the mountain. Since the mountain slopes downhill and the trail is simply crossing that slope, we found ourselves leaning to the left much of the time.

Once we entered the forest, the trail began a steep descent. There were more rocks to bounce over and even some old mining camps to explore, but nothing to test our 4-wheeling expertise.

The best surviving cabin along the way was at the edge of the forest in a meadow. It would not exactly be a good place to go to get out of the rain, but it is in a location some of us might like to call, "home".

Judging by the slope, we began to believe there would be nothing more to the Glacier Ridge Trail than a lot of beautiful scenery.

Then we came to a spot where the trail dropped off so suddenly, I could not see it over the hood. I opened the door, stepped out and looked over the edge. A smile formed on my lips as I reached for the mic. "Looks like this is gonna be fun! It's a real **Axle Crusher!**"

As with any threatening trail, we walked down, then back up carefully planning our approach. "A rock here. Another rock there. we'll be out of here in time for supper .... Okay. ... So, it may be a late supper."

The rough section was not more than a couple hundred yards long, but it was nearly vertical and the boulders were huge.

I inched the Rocky down little by little with Dusty directing me all the way. He watched the under-carriage to be sure I would not get high centered as the Rocky moved step by step to the bottom. If it looked like I might get hung up, we would pile rocks in front of the tires to give them something to fall onto without taking the full step all at once. Don't be fooled by the photos. They don't even begin to do justice for the angle of this trail.

Finally, the Rocky was all the way down. I started hiking uphill with Dusty at my side. "Well, son. It's your turn."

He stopped in his tracks. "You want me to (gulp) drive down that?"

"There's a first time for everything and it's time for you to tackle a VDL Trail."

"What if I break the truck?"

"If you break it ... you fix it."

I guided him down the trail the same as he had done for me. On trails like this one, the spotter is actually the one driving the truck.

From inside, everything looks and feels different than it actually is. Many times, the driver will stop and get out just because the direction his spotter is telling him to go, does not feel right. After a quick glance from outside the vehicle, he will get back in and do what his spotter told him to do in the first place.

The Glacier Ridge Trail does have a bad spot in it. There most definitely is a good chance to damage a vehicle. Some folks will turn around at the top of Axle Crusher and go back the way they came in.

A "One Way! Do Not Enter!" sign once stood at the point where the Glacier Ridge Trail connects to the Middle Fork Swan Trail. The last time we were there, it was gone.

OUTLAW AND DUSTY

GLACIER RIDGE NAVIGATION

The following odometer readings were taken using a '97 Isuzu Trooper. The GPS positions were acquired by referencing Google Maps.

ODO	Latitude N	Longitude W	Landmarks and descriptions
0.0	39.377516	105.800501	Begin in the town of Jefferson. Reset trip meter and turn north on Michigan Creek Road.
5.9	39.411680	105.884508	Follow signs to Michigan creek Campground. Pay to stay.
11.9	39.458054	105.916595	This is Georgia Pass. Take the right fork (258). To the three way.

The three-way intersection is obvious. Right goes to a campsite. Middle goes to Glacier Peak but is closed. Left goes to Axle Crusher. It is about six miles to the Middle Fork Swan trail. Montezuma is right. Breckenridge is left.

MOSQUITO PASS

HIGHWAY OF FROZEN DEATH

An undetermined number of would-be miners lost their lives attempting to cross Mosquito Pass during the winter.

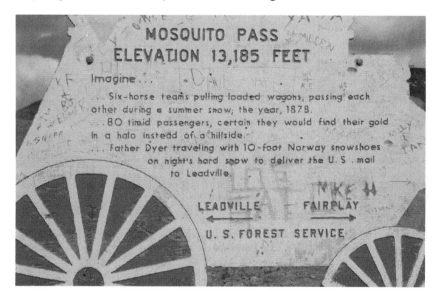

They were the ones who came from the East ... the ones without "Mountain Savvy" ... the ones who were totally unprepared for the ferocious blizzards that would greet them. They paid for an education they could never use, because they paid for it with their lives. And so, the road over Mosquito Pass was named the, "Highway of Frozen Death".

It was more than a hundred years ago that prospectors began moving into Mosquito Gulch. They discovered enough ore to encourage more to come in hopes that the motherload was only a few feet deeper.

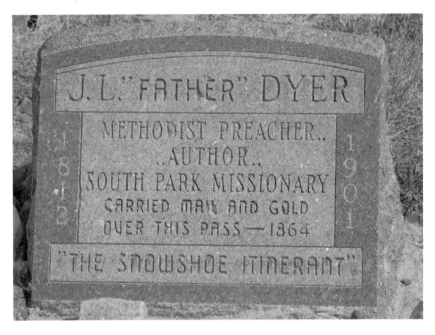

Little by little, the population in the gulch grew until they realized they were becoming a town. A town has to be called something ... but what would they call theirs. Being true individualists, as most pioneers were, they just could not agree on anything.

How about, "Camp Sterling"? They tried it for a while, but something just wasn't right.

How about, "Sterling City? Naw. It needs to be unique."

And so, a special meeting was called. They were determined to settle the name problem permanently, no matter how long it took.

After all, their little community had grown to more than 250 residents!

As the group secretary turned to the minutes of the last meeting, he suddenly exclaimed, "Thar's a dang blamed musquito squished flatter thun uh flapjack in the middle of the minutes!"

(Okay. So maybe that's not an exact quote.)

They all began to chuckle. It appeared Mother Nature had named their small town for them. She had even entered it in the minutes. All they needed was a final vote.

Whoops! There was one more problem. No one at the meeting knew how to spell the little critter. After some debate, the newly named town was christened, "MUSQUITO".

But, there was not enough wealth around Musquito to keep it going. Little by little it began to fade. Mines began closing. Miners moved away.

Then, suddenly, ORO CITY (Later named Leadville) took off with a bang and Musquito found it was conveniently positioned right in the path of the most direct route between Denver and Oro City.

It was instantly revived as a supply point, stage stop, and relay station for travelers headed over Mosquito Pass.

Musquito thrived until a new railway bypassed it and provided easier passage than the dangerous pass road. A few years later, nothing was left but dust and brush.

In the beginning, Mosquito Pass was no more than a mule trail, far too dangerous for wagons, but as the traffic increased, the trail was widened into a road and became one of the busiest roads in the state. Its reputation as the Highway of Frozen Death did not stop those who were inflicted with gold fever.

One of those who saw Mosquito Pass at its worst and lived to tell the story was to be known as "Chicken Bill". He was a man who recognized opportunity when he saw it.

"Them miners been livin' all winter on venison stew and bully beef. I'll bet they'd pay a hefty price for a nice plump chicken."

With that thought, he bought up all the foul he could find and, with the first break in spring weather, headed up Mosquito Pass.

During the night, a typical Mosquito Pass springtime storm caught Bill with nowhere to go. When the morning sun finally came, he found his chickens were all frozen solid.

Bill was not easily beaten. He simply plucked the chickens and stuffed them full of snow to keep them frozen. A few hours later, the miners were frying up the chickens and Chicken Bill was stuffing his pockets with gold.

There were other fortunes made in Leadville without digging for it. When Western Union completed its line over Mosquito Pass around 1878, the first newspaper came to life. Its editors received coded news bits from Denver. If anything was garbled up too badly, they just filled it in with what they thought sounded right. After all, who was to know what the truth was anyway. On its first day, the little paper sold over 9000 copies.

With a market like that, nothing could stop the flow of information over those lines. If a storm blew them down, the paper's editors would join Western Union crews through blinding snow storms and paralyzing cold to make the repairs.

"Mr. Watson, come here. I want you." Remember those words out of your history books. Less than three years after they were uttered, the first telephone wires were stretched over Mosquito Pass. It was the only telephone line in the world built at such high altitude.

Today, Mosquito Pass can be traveled in any high clearance vehicle with low range gearing. It is rocky, and narrow in places, but normally in good condition. Snow drifts keep it closed most of the year but late August and September usually work. It is sometimes open in July and occasionally an early snow storm will close it in September. Take a shovel just in case.

There are several side trails off the main road. Some of them lead to old mining camps, others go to lakes, and one ends at the site of an old tramway. When you go to Mosquito Pass, plan on an entire day so you can make the side trips.

Happy Trails!

MOSQUITO PASS NAVIGATION

The following odometer readings were taken using a '97 Isuzu Trooper.
The GPS positions were acquired by referencing Google Maps.
Not all could be found.

ODO	Latitude N	Longitude W	Landmarks and descriptions
0.0	39.221539	105.993627	Reset meter or note mileage in Fairplay at the intersection of 285 and 9.
3.8	39.270470	106.047360	Turn left and follow Park County 12. Which is the Mosquito Pass Road.
7.4			The town of Park City is small.
9.5			"Y" intersection. Go right.
10.7			Intersection. Go straight.
11.9			Straight. The trail on the right goes up to old mines.
12.6			Straight. The trail on the right goes to a lake.
13.6			Straight. The trail on the left goes back down the mountain but is normally closed.
14.7	39.281069	106.186197	Mosquito Pass.

The trail behind the sign goes to Mosquito Peak and is for foot travel only. Notice the memorial for Father Dyer.

Follow County Road 3 down the mountain to the creek crossing. This is the runoff for Evans Gulch Number 2 Reservoir. Gates are locked.

| 17.9/0 | 39.259619 | 106.218520 | After crossing the creek, turn right keeping the gate behind you. |

Follow the main road into Leadville and you will be on Harrison St.

GETTING LOST IN STYLE

Mosquito crosses over the Continental Divide. The east side is in the Pike National Forest and the west side is in the San Isabel National Forest. The Pike map is more detailed showing Cooney Lake and Park City, but does not include Leadville. The USGS Park County #1 map is very detailed and handy to have while exploring the east side of the pass.

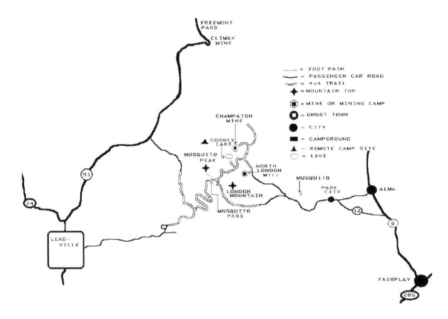

HAGERMAN PASS

11960 FEET IN ELEVATION

Getting from one side of the Great Divide to the other created many challenges for early residents of Colorado. Especially when the vehicle being used was a train. The crossing west of Leadville was one of the busiest.

NOTE: The photos used in the original book for Hagerman Pass could not be found. Even worse, the digital copies we have were not in the required 300 DPI quality. We have tried to convert them and only have the small images you find below.

During the 1980's the NFS allowed the water board to plow the road over Hagerman but that is no longer an option.	There were many trestles for the railroad to the Hagerman Tunnel. The one that was here was a long one.

Rails were laid westward until they pointed directly at the wall of a mountain. The town of Douglass City was erected and engineers began moving in. They were skilled in the building of magnificent trestles and rugged snow sheds. They blasted through solid rock and filled in sagging valleys to form a steadily ascending railroad pointed directly at the side of the mountain.

They blasted the Hagerman Tunnel through a half mile of solid rock to the west side of the Great Divide. Upon its completion, that was the highest railroad tunnel in the world and the 1,084-foot curved wooden trestle leading to it was an engineering wonder.

The story written on the Douglass City marker has faded beyond recognition.	The streets of Douglass City can still be found but only one cabin still resists the brutal weather.

The construction crews were a hardy bunch and their temporary home was named Douglass City. It's one street was lined with eight saloons (mostly in tents) and a dance hall. Its ladies of the evening were no doubt as tough as the men who supported them with the money they earned working in the eleven-thousand-foot-high elements. Its reputation was that of a wild town where men went to drink and gamble ... but often ended up fighting and dying. It was truly a town where only the strong survived. That was then. This is now.

Harsh winters, treasure hunters, and vandals will eventually wipe out all that remains of Douglass City. Don't be a part of the problem. Take nothing but pictures. Leave nothing but footprints.

Getting to Douglass City requires walking along the old railroad grade and up a side trail. It is a 45-minute walk at a steady pace, but is worth every step.

Follow the main street up the side of the hill to a small lake and the remains of more buildings. There are even a few shaky telegraph poles still standing. The trail goes up the hill through scattered lumber left behind by a fallen snow shed. The Hagerman Tunnel is still open, but **signs warn you not to enter it**.

The view from the mouth of the tunnel was and still is magnificent. As you stand with your back to the tunnel, you get the same view the locomotive engineers saw every time they exited its total darkness.

At this point, a valley was cut for the track	This east end of Hagerman tunnel can be reached using the hiking trail
At this point the mountain had to be sliced open to keep the railbed level.	**The Hagerman tunnel on the east side can only be accessed using the hiking trial.**

We recommend taking the long way back to the vehicles. The two-hour walk is more like a stroll most of the way since you will be following the gradual descent of the original railroad bed. It takes you by Hagerman Lake, (Looks like a good fishing spot), and through man-made canyons that were necessary to continue the gradual grade. You'll walk up to the end of where the wooden trestles spanned long valleys.

The Colorado Midland Railway was never profitable. Despite its marvelous engineering feats, it was just too high in the mountains. Snow closed it more than it was open and maintenance was just too costly. It lasted about three years.

In 1891, the two-mile-long Carlton Tunnel was blasted through the mountain at an elevation 600-feet lower than the Hagerman Tunnel. The higher passage was permanently closed. The Carlton Tunnel also proved to be too costly to maintain and was abandoned by the railroad. It was reopened in 1924 and used until 1937 as a passenger car route. A few years later, it became a water diversion passage. A huge pipeline was installed from end to end. The Ivanhoe lake feeds the pipeline and the water begins a long journey to Colorado Springs. That pipeline is still in use. Caretakers use the buildings on the west end to provide year-round maintenance.

You will drive by the Carlton Tunnel on the way to where the Hagerman Trail begins. It is sealed and offers very little in the way of something to look at.

Any time I see a tunnel, the first thing I want to know is "Where's the other end?" We already mentioned that both tunnels go to the other side of the Great Divide. It should be no surprise that if you want to see the other end, you must cross the 11,982-foot pass that takes you over the top. In past years, the trail was opened by the Colorado Springs Water Department in time for Memorial Day, however, the National Forest Service decided the pass should melt naturally so it is rarely open now until late July.

From the summit of the pass, continue down the western slope until you come to a "T" in the road. At that point, a sign points behind you and says you were on Road 105. Another sign says you are about to get on Road 527. If you were to turn right, you would go by Ruedi Reservoir and eventually (like the trains that used the tunnels) arrive in Basalt, Co.

Turn left and follow the road to just past the dam for Ivanhoe Lake. The railroad used to travel right down the middle of where the lake is today, and if the water is low enough, you can still see the railbed going across the lake. If you follow that railbed toward the mountain, it will lead you to the west end of the Carlton Tunnel which is on the east end of the lake.

Check with the caretaker before visiting the tunnel. We were told that access to the tunnel is open to the public but the tunnel itself may not be entered. It is boarded up and dangerous, but if you have some battery-operated spotlights like we use, it sure is interesting to shine a light between the boards to light up the inside and admire the wooden frame that was built to hold the ceiling up. Without entering the tunnel, you can see where the ceiling has caved in.

The trail behind the entrance to the Carlton Tunnel follows another railbed to the west entrance of the Hagerman Tunnel.

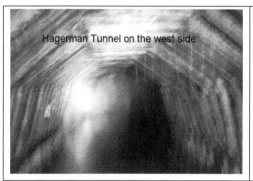
Hagerman Tunnel on the west side

The tunnel entrance has caved in, however, if you climb the mountain wall, you can find a suitable place to shine your battery-operated spotlight inside. Once again, the framework is a real piece of art. Don't enter the tunnel though. It has about eight feet of water in it and it could come tumbling down at any time.

HAGERMAN PASS NAVIGATION

From Leadville, turn west on 6th. street. Follow it to the "T" in the road and turn right. Continue past Sugar Loafin' Campground, past the intersection for Turquoise Lake Portal, through the next intersection, and over the dam. About 3 miles past the dam is a dirt road going left. Follow it around the lake to Carlton Tunnel. There is a parking area there for hikers and fishermen who hike up to Windsor Lake. About one mile past the tunnel is the hiking trail to Douglass City and Hagerman Tunnel. The old railbed is easy to see and even easier to follow. The 4X4 trail continues a steady climb to the summit of the pass.

GETTING LOST IN STYLE

The maps for the area are the USGS Topo maps of Lake County and Pitkin County number 2. You can find Hagerman and Carlton Tunnels quite easily by first looking for Turquoise Lake on the Lake County map. Both tunnels are on the west end of the lake. The Pitkin map is needed to find the other end of the tunnels across the Great Divide. You can also find both tunnels on the San Isabel National Forest Map and on the White River National Forest Map. We prefer the White River because it shows the entire trail from Leadville to Basalt.

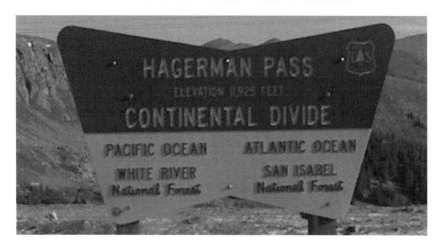

HAGERMAN PASS MAP

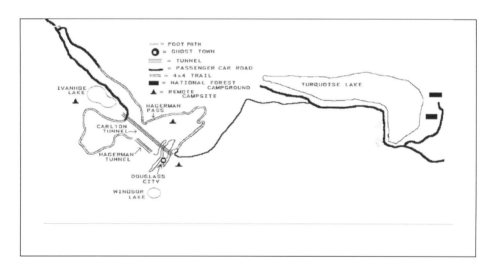

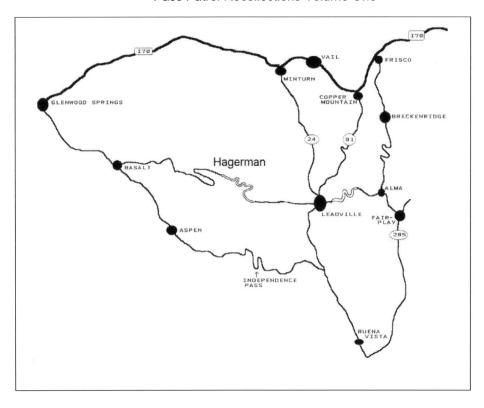

TAYLOR PASS

11928 FEET IN ELEVATION

During the early 1880s, a thriving city sprung up west of the Continental Divide. It was called Ashcroft.

It's located a short distance from Aspen.

During its better days, it had a telegraph line, stagecoach service, and even a school.

Ashcroft was a busy mining town before Aspen was anything more than a few scattered shacks. In the beginning, the only way to get supplies into Ashcroft was over Taylor Pass. A few years later, Pearl Pass was open from Crested Butte which increased traffic through Ashcroft.

Eventually, a trail was cut over Independence Pass and that became the favored route. Traffic through Ashcroft dwindled away. Most of its residents simply packed up and moved to the location where Aspen is today.

When Ashcroft died, Taylor Pass and Pearl Pass were mostly abandoned. Both are 4X4 trails now. We usually bundle them together as a week-end trip. Pearl is frequently blocked by snow drifts until Labor Day.

Our journey normally begins in Buena Vista. We follow the same route the supply wagons used. A graded gravel road takes us over Cottonwood Pass into Taylor Park. We then follow the banks of Taylor Reservoir to the site of the ghost town of Bowman.

Bowman used to be a supply point and stagecoach stop. It was a point of no return for those who might change their minds about making the difficult journey over Taylor Pass. Weather conditions, and the Ute Indians, were more than enough to cause some to reconsider.

A small sign is all that's left of Bowman. The next sign on the road points to Taylor Pass. The trail begins as a bumpy ride through the forest. There are great camping spots and some fishing along the way.

At one point, the trail follows the creek, or the creek follows the trail. Either way, you can be bumper deep in water during spring run-off.

About the time the trail climbs above timberline, you'll find Taylor Lake. It is a favorite fishing spot for lots of folks. You'll see the near vertical trail that was once our favorite route to the summit of the pass. It was closed during 1988 and a rocky path with a more gradual slope was cut around it.

The summit of the pass is a beautiful place to breathe in some clean, cool, fresh Colorado air. The view of the valleys and mountains from that point is one of the best in the state.

If you were going to Ashcroft about 100 years ago, you would need to disassemble your wagon at the summit. There was no road so you lowered it down piece by piece to the bottom of the ledge on that side. Fortunately, a ledge trail was built to eliminate that minor inconvenience. I have often wondered why they didn't just park another wagon at the bottom, lower the goods into it, and take it the rest of the way to Ashcroft. The last person I asked, said, "Maybe they only had one wagon."

"Hm-m-m-m."

The Ashcroft side of Taylor Pass is a car road and an easy cruise. There is a lot of private property and mining claims along the way, so stay on the road. After you cross the creek, turn right onto the main road to reach Aspen. Ashcroft and Pearl Pass are both to the left.

BY THE WAY

"Oh! I almost forgot. For those of you who are slightly dated … mature is a better word. You might remember the long-ago TV series called, "Sergeant Preston of the Yukon." That series was filmed in Ashcroft. Just thought you might like to know.

GETTING LOST IN STYLE

The Gunnison National Forest Map covers the area well. The USGS maps of the area are Gunnison Cty #3 and Pitkin Cty #2.

NAVIGATION FOR TAYLOR PASS

The following odometer readings were taken using a '97 Isuzu Trooper.
The GPS positions were acquired by referencing Google Maps.

ODO	Latitude N	Longitude W	Landmarks & other locations

Turn west at the sign for Cottonwood Pass in downtown Buena Vista. Follow the road about 38 miles to Taylor Reservoir where the road forms a T at the stop sign. Turn right at that intersection and begin the directions below.

ODO	Latitude N	Longitude W	Landmarks & other locations
0.0	38.840952	106.557341	Right at T intersection at the reservoir.
4.1/0	38.894709	106.570136	Stay on FSR742. Road to right is Pie Plant ghost town. Reset trip meter.
10.7	38.995679	106.703427	Turn at the sign for Taylor Pass.
14.1/0	39.017321	106.749354	Both routes to around Taylor Lake. The right fork is shorter.
1.5	39.020017	106.755078	This is Taylor Pass. 11,928 feet in elevation.

The left fork is an easy road going 5 miles to the intersection for Ashcroft and Aspen. The right fork goes to Aspen and is more scenic.

TAYLOR PASS MAP

The following map displays the general area with nearby cities for orientation.

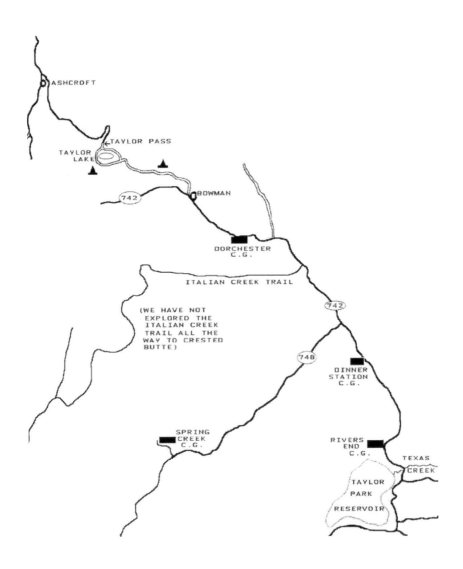

The map below is an expanded view of Taylor Pass. It is a small part of the preceding map.

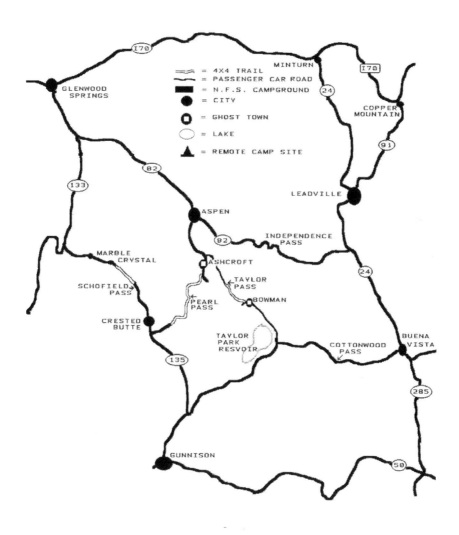

PEARL PASS

This trip occurred in September of 1985 and first published in 1986. The photos are from different trips including 1990.

Of all the passes in Colorado, there is one that holds a special meaning to me. It was the first 4X4 trail that taught me:

"It's not nice to fool with Mother Nature!"

I swore to her that if she would just let me live, I would sell my 4X4 and never be seen outside the city limits again. Of course, all women know men can't be trusted to keep such promises so, when I broke it, she did not come after me with the wrath of a woman scorned. Like most women, she just tucked that promise away in a little hidden location so she could bring it out to get even at every opportunity.

Once upon a time ... long, long ago ... on my second trip to the Colorado mountains ... in a 1979 Bronco ... I thought I was gonna die!

I was new to Colorado, and not at all experienced with mountain 4-wheeling. Tackling Pearl Pass was probably a little too ambitious for me at that time, but when Mother Nature started picking on me, I was in way over my head.

The morning had included an uneventful, but enjoyable, trip over Taylor Pass. Although the weather looked and felt threatening, we decided to tackle Pearl. No one in our group of three vehicles had ever been over Pearl Pass before, so we were, "Boldly going where we had never gone before."

The climb toward the pass was a tough one. There were lots of sharp rocks everywhere and the trail leaned toward the cliff at a steep angle.

"Breaker 13! The Bronco's gotta flat tire!" Rick was following me and noticed the tire from behind. His call over the CB radio was not a welcome message.

We stepped out of the vehicles and immediately reached back inside for jackets. The wind was picking up, the sky was nearly black, and Mother Nature wasn't even serious yet.

I walked around to the passenger side and got a real shock. Both tires on that side of the vehicle were flat and already off the rims. That was my first lesson in Pass Patrol's School of Hard Knocks.

"Don't take a full-sized vehicle into the mountains on city tires."

We took the spare off the Bronco and another off the Jeep to get the Bronco up off the rocks.

So ... there we were. At the crest of Pearl Pass. Pushing our way through an axle deep snow drift left over from last winter ... on a ledge road barely wide enough to support a full-sized vehicle ... and the only spare tire we had left would only fit a Nissan.

A roar of thunder echoed through the mountains. "Mother Nature is laughing at us."

She began throwing water on us. Very cold water ... with a dash of snow mixed in just for flavor.

"We better get outta here," Bob said as he rushed toward his Nissan pickup. "If this freezes, we'll be camping up here all night."

We started down the trail toward Crested Butte. The light rain became a downpour. It continuously picked up in intensity.

The ledge trail dropped below tree line. Roads that were dusty a few hours earlier where transformed into mud. The vehicles inched along, occasionally slipping dangerously close to the cliff's edge as muddy tires tried desperately to cling to slick rocks.

"Breaker 13. The Nissan's got a flat on the right rear."

"This just can't be happening," we thought. How can any group get three flat tires? By the time we got the Nissan back up in the air, we were all soaked. We cranked up the heaters in the vehicles and pushed onward.

We were tired and concerned about Mother Nature. The clouds were so thick, we might as well have been traveling at night. I inched the Bronco up onto a big rock and felt it slip to the right with a hard, "Bang!"

"Breaker 13. The Bronco's high centered."

Rick hurried forward and tied a tow strap onto the Bronco. He shoved his Jeep in reverse and roared backwards, but the Jeep stopped like it hit a wall. Pulling a Bronco with a little Jeep is like David tugging on Goliath. Nothing happened.

We jacked the Bronco up and put rocks under the tires to give it height. When we let the Bronco down, it was barely touching the rock. I expected it to easily slip off the rock under power, but instead, the muddy tires slipped on the rocks. I could hear the familiar hissing of a tire losing air.

"You just sliced another tire," Bob announced. "You better get it off that rock now or it'll be there forever!"

I shoved it into gear and floored the gas pedal. The Bronco lunged off the rock and came to a stop near the edge of another drop-off. I was standing on the brakes to keep it from sliding over the edge when I realized ... the trail went over that edge.

In front of the vehicle was a gully and only way down the hill was to straddle its center. The walls of the gully were steep and extremely slippery. By driving the tires of the vehicle on each of the two walls, the center of the gully could be avoided, but there would be enough space under the vehicle to walk under and change the oil.

So, there I was. Sitting at the edge of a muddy drop-off ... three hours from the nearest city ... with three flat tires ... a half tank of gas, wearing sun glasses and a cowboy hat. "YEEEE HAAAWWW!"

I was going downhill and picking up speed ... with the brakes locked up! My left rear tire came off the rim and beat me to the bottom of the hill! The Bronco stopped sideways in the trail at the bottom. I eased it onto a level area between some trees and turned off the engine. That ride was over!

We took four rims off the Bronco and tossed them into the back of the Nissan. We managed to get five of us into the king cab but it was not comfortable. The rain continued to beat down steadily. All sunlight was gone. We had mud from the tips of our toes to just over our eyebrows. We still had many miles of trail to cover with no idea of what to expect.

That's when I made that promise to Mother Nature.

"If I ever get this Bronco out of here, I'll sell it and never leave the city limits again!"

We reached Crested Butte about 8 p.m. In those days, nothing was open in that city after dark. We went to Gunnison, but only found one tire shop open. They had two used tires that would fit a Bronco. One of them was bald. We decided it was time to retreat and form a new battle plan.

When our group stepped into the Pizza Hut, the music stopped. Waitresses hid behind managers and managers backed into corners. We looked like the walking dead. Mud was on our clothes, in our hair, and even on our faces. We were hungry.

Rick's wife wiped a clump of mud from her cheek and gave the manager a look that dared him to run us off. "Table for eight."

Suddenly, everybody began hustling to get the tables set up. The music started and the other customers turned back to their own meals. We were determined to be harmless.

We drove to Grand Junction that night and stayed at Bob's house. The next day, I bought a full set of six ply tires. We tossed them into the back of the Nissan and headed for Pearl. The rain had stopped. The sky was clear. And the forest was beautiful. Mother Nature had finished teasing us and had, no doubt, gone off to play with some other unprepared rookies.

We put the tires on the Bronco and headed for home. "Breaker 13! The Jeep's gotta flat on the left rear."

"That's okay. We got lots of tires!

Pearl is always ready for lunch and its favorite meal is 4X4s. When it's not eating four ply tires, it's ripping away at oil pans. We once followed a trail of oil to a 4X4 with a ruined engine. I'm sure the driver thought he had a good reason for driving the vehicle until it was completely out of oil, but his decision to do so was an expensive one.

The other side of the story concerns the most beautiful, breathtaking, mountain scenery Pearl Pass has to offer. It is the ideal trail for those who are very patient, like to fish, like to camp, or just enjoy poking along and breathing clean country air. Those people keep going back to the high mountain lakes, the clear bubbling streams, the roaring waterfalls, and the dense isolated forest.

It's nearly thirty miles from Ashcroft to Crested Butte by way of Pearl Pass and, even in dry weather, it is 4-WHEELING all the way. There is plenty of rock crawling, lots of narrow shelf road, and numerous creek crossings. In the spring, those creeks can be door handle deep, but that's when the fishing is at its best.

Pearl Pass began as a wagon road to get supplies between Ashcroft and Crested Butte. The most challenging direction to travel Pearl is to begin in Ashcroft.

Ashcroft is an old ghost town from the days of gold fever. It was a thriving city before Aspen was anything more than a tent camp. Ashcroft has been used in movies so its buildings are still in pretty good condition.

One other thing you should know is that Pearl Pass is seldom open. Some years the snow never melts off the top of the Pass. Other years it's open for a few weeks in late August or early September. Take a shovel and open it for us while you're there.

PEARL PASS NAVIGATION

The following odometer readings were taken using a '97 Isuzu Trooper.
The GPS positions were acquired by referencing Google Maps.

West of Aspen, use the roundabout to get on Castle Creek Road. It's the that goes past the hospital.			
ODO	**Latitude N**	**Longitude W**	**Landmarks and descriptions**
0.0	39.195138	106.840144	Use the roundabout to get onto Castle Creek Road.
Take Castle Creek Rd which is County Road 15.			
10.3	39.060168	106.800902	Stay on Road 15. Road on left goes to Taylor Pass.
10.6/0	39.055640	106.799673	Parking for hike into Ashcroft. Reset Trip Meter.
1.6/0	39.029208	106.807851	Right on FSR 102 is the beginning of the road to Pearl Pass.
2.8	39.005486	106.838193	Left at Pearl Pass Sign.
7.0	38.979438	106.823792	Pearl Pass Summit. It's still 17 miles to Crested Butte.

GETTING LOST IN STYLE

The Gunnison National Forest Map covers the area pretty well. The USGS maps of the area are Gunnison County #3 and Pitkin County #2.

PEARL PASS MAP

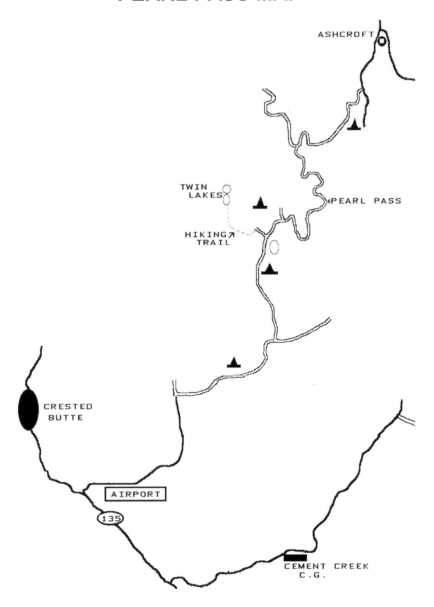

ASHCROFT

TWIN
LAKES

← PEARL PASS

HIKING
TRAIL

CRESTED
BUTTE

AIRPORT

135

CEMENT CREEK
C.G.

SCHOFIELD PASS

It tops out at 10,707 feet, and the view along the Crystal River is beautiful. During the year of 1880, Ulysses S. Grant spent a lot of time in the area, visiting many towns on both sides of the Pass.

We have gone over it in both directions, however, it is easier to go from Crested Butte to Marble than in the other direction. The ghost town of Gothic north of Crested Butte has become a major tourist attraction. During the summer months, it is bursting at the seams with groups of people. Hikers, bikers, campers, 4-wheelers, sportsmen, and even people who didn't really get there on purpose are wandering around everywhere.

NOTE: The photos used in the original book for Schofield Pass could not be found. Even worse, the digital copies we have were not in the required 300 DPI quality. We have tried to convert them and only have the small images you find below. The story remains the same with minor edits for quality.

After finishing Pearl Pass, we drove to the summit of Schofield Pass on a graded road. The north side is narrow and rocky.

Imagining Gothic the way it began is easier during the summer months when all the people are there, but you'll wonder where they all go after dark.

During the time Grant was visiting the area, Gothic's population was rising on its way to a peak of 8,000 and its reputation was one of a party town where women dared to wear their skirts all the way up to their knees. Gambling, drinking, and shady ladies were as common as having pockets full of gold and silver. Gothic was referred to as the richest town in Gunnison County.

Gothic was in the fast lane and the old saying, "Live fast - Die young!" best describes what happened. It was almost like someone threw a party so everybody came, but when the party was over, everybody left. Before the mid-1880s, Gothic was virtually abandoned.

Gothic's five-year party was not all fun and games. Many who came, are still there ... buried after the high mountain elements took their lives. Each year, winter came and winter went ... taking rookie miners with it. Avalanches were common in those days, and still are today. The trail over Schofield Pass is frequently closed for years at a time by avalanches.

The trail is very narrow in places.	Navigating the rocks and the edge of the cliff.

Schofield is an easy road until it gets to the Crystal River. From there on, it is a killer. This intimidating little trail took the lives of a whole car load of folks several years back. There are different versions of exactly what happened on that horrible day and I have not investigated the incident to see which version is the most accurate. When you're standing on top ... looking down ... it really doesn't matter who's right. The fact is, this trail has done claimed the lives of at least one family.

"It darn sure ain't gonna get mine! Out'ta the truck!"

The way I heard it, a brand-new Suburban was on its way up when the driver decided to step out and take a picture. If this version is true, I cannot even imagine the horror that man must have experienced when the vehicle popped out of PARK and shot backwards over the cliff, plunging into the paralyzing cold water of Devil's Punchbowl.

According to legend, it's all caused by a Ute Curse placed on the area when the Utes were driven out. Those who challenge the curse, must be prepared to endure its wrath. Curse or no curse, there is a page in the unwritten bible of Outlaw's Code titled, "Thou shalt not endanger the lives of thy passengers. Make'um walk."

The trail is a FAT MAN'S MISERY for full-size vehicles. Every time I do it in a full-size truck, I swear to put the thing on a low-octane diet as soon as I get back. Don't be distracted by the beauty of the canyon. If you stop to take pictures, make sure your vehicle will be there when you get back. Turn off the engine, turn the wheels toward the wall, and set your emergency brake ... tight. If you have an automatic, do not put your faith in PARK. If you have standard shift, leave it in reverse.

The surface of the trail is rough and rocky. Although going down Crystal Canyon is easier than going up, there are some places where you might drag the undercarriage. From the bridge to Crystal, the road becomes very rough and earns its difficult rating. From Crystal to Marble is a little better but there won't be much time for daydreaming.

Overall, the Schofield Pass Trail is more intimidating than it is dangerous ... partly because of its past history. It appears to threaten your every move, yet there is room for a full-size vehicle to get through with a "little bit of room to spare."

The bridge across the Crystal River is barely wide enough for a full-size vehicle. The vehicle above is on the way down the trail to Marble and the one on the right is on the way to Schofield Pass.

Those of you who shy away from ledge trails and drop-offs, will most definitely be frightened by this trail.

The Crystal Mill on the Crystal River is said to be one of the most photographed locations in Colorado. You can find it on calendars and souvenirs everywhere.

As you can see in the photo, most of the dam is gone and the old building is feeling its years.

Unfortunately, we will probably lose this trail in the next few years. Every year, those who think roads are to walk on, attempt to close it down.

Every year, the Crystal Mill becomes a little more unsteady. Perhaps someone will stabilize it.

Thanks to the CA4WDC and some other concerned citizens, previous efforts to close it have been defeated, but the Forest Service is under constant pressure to put gates on both ends. Unless we 4-wheelers continue to write letters with the opposing view, those gates will eventually be installed.

The argument in favor of closing Schofield Pass is, "It's dangerous" ... but then so is driving through Denver. In both cases, if you are careful and do what should be done, there won't be any trouble!

GETTING LOST IN STYLE

The Gunnison National Forest Map and the USGS Gunnison County #1 & #2 include the area for Schofield Pass.

SCHOFIELD PASS NAVIGATION

Through Marble & Crystal to Schofield Pass

The following odometer readings were taken using a '97 Isuzu Trooper.
The GPS positions were acquired by referencing Google Maps.

About 20 miles south of Carbondale, Colorado on Highway 133 is the turnoff for Marble onto County Road 3. You will be on CR 3 all the way to the National Forest Boundary.

ODO	Latitude N	Longitude W	Landmarks and descriptions
0.0	39.115934	107.270683	Turn off Highway 133 between mile posts 46 & 47.
5.8	39.072686	107.181684	Follow County Rd 3 to Marble.

It is the main road through town. Leave town at Beaver Lake.

7.9	39.074833	107.159123	Right. Left is Lead King Basin.
8.2	39.071322	107.155141	Lizard Lake.
11.5	39.059227	107.104767	Crystal Mill.
12.3/0	39.059249	107.096414	Right fork. Reset trip meter.

Left is another road to Lead King Basin. At this point, County Rd 3 ends and Forest Road 317 begins. The road is closed at this point in from September to July of each year.

| 1.3 | 39.049912 | 107.077768 | This is the bridge in the story |

It crosses over the South Fork of the Crystal River. Devil's Punchbowl is visible from the bridge.

| 4.5 | 39.016105 | 107.047464 | Stay on FS 317. Pass is ahead |

It goes to Schofield Pass and Crested Butte. Top of pass is 10,707 ft.

| 10.1 | 38.957788 | 106.988890 | Gothic. |

It's like St. Elmo. It has never actually been a ghost town.

| 17.7 | 38.868029 | 106.980852 | Stop sign in Crested Butte. |

SCHOFIELD PASS MAP

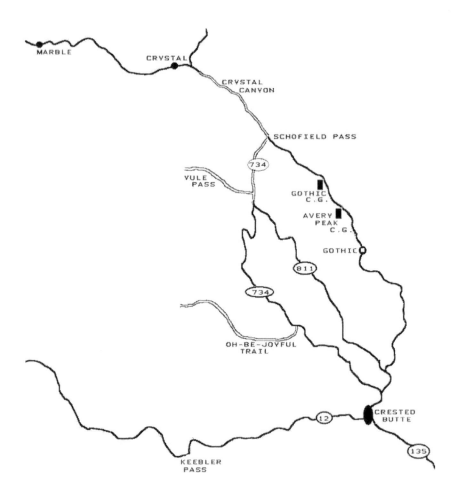

MARY MURPHY MINE
AND ROMLEY GHOST TOWN

Mary Murphy must have been a very special nurse. A certain prospector, who was under her care in a Denver hospital for a while, was so impressed, he went back to the mountains and staked a claim with her name on it.

After some rocky starts, that claim became the largest mine in the Alpine district. Three towns: St. Elmo, Romley, and Hancock, were born and died with the Mary Murphy Mine. Romley was the closest to the mine and parts of it can still be found along the road between St. Elmo and the Alpine Tunnel.

Romley's purpose was to serve the Mary Murphy Mine. It was built on both sides of the railway and a 5000-foot tramway was built up Pomeroy Gulch so the ore could be lowered from the mine to the rail cars. Much of that tramway and the buildings that supported it are still standing.

A rocky road follows the tramway from the railway to the headquarters for the mine pictured below.

That section of the road is in good enough condition for two-wheel drive vehicles, but the grade is steep.

Along the way is a very interesting two-story log cabin with the floor of the upper level still in place. It sits in a perfect location right on the banks of a rumbling mountain stream.

The most important of all the buildings is the one where all the paperwork was done. This old one-hole seater truly tested the theory that "--it really does roll downhill."

The view from the privy is straight up the mountain to a building that still houses some old tramway machinery. There is a side trail leading to the area above that building, but it is reserved for those who have no common sense ... like me.

The trail scales the mountain wall almost all the way to the top where the Mary Murphy Mine was located. That section of the trail is extremely narrow ... with lots of emphasis on the word "narrow". The first time I tried to get up there, I was in a full-sized Bronco, which spectators quickly named, "Casper - the soon to be ghost."

Nothing was going well that day. We had been chased all over the Alpine District by thunderstorms, and we could see another one coming up Pomeroy Gulch from Romley. But, if there was even the slightest remote chance we could make it all the way to the top, we just had to try. After all, we were, "Boldly going where we had never gone before!"

Except for squeezing between some paint-abusive brush on both sides of the trail, it started out okay. Just beyond the brush, the trail became … not so okay … real fast. We made it about half way up the mountain with slightly more than standing room on either side of the Bronco, and came to a place where the distance from the outside of my driver's side tire to the sheer drop-off was less than three inches.

"You're okay on this side," John whispered with a nervous grin while clinging to the passenger-side door handle. A huge boulder on the right was keeping the vehicle from getting any closer to the wall and we were not sure how long the three-inch ledge on the left was going to be there with two tons of Bronco resting on it.

Suddenly, there was a blast of lightning and a crack of thunder that seemed to shake the whole truck. I looked out the window and watched little pebbles leave the trail's edge and head quickly down the near-vertical hillside to the valley floor far … far below.

Then, another blast of lightning and deafening thunder that hit so close we thought we were going to be fried.

"Hey! I can take a hint," I said while nervously reaching for that all-saving reverse gear. "Don't mess with Mother Nature. She's still upset over that promise on Pearl Pass."

Backing down a half mile of narrow-ledge trail is not on my ten favorite things to do in a thunderstorm ... or any other time since we're on the subject ... but I am pleased to announce that we made it and Casper did not become a ghost.

We returned the following year with a Jeep and a Ford Ranger. Even in the smaller vehicles, the trip was very interesting but the trail ended before getting to the top. That was the last time we visited the ledge trail although we get out to Pomeroy Lake nearly every year.

At the point where the trail leaves the headquarters for Pomeroy Lake, it becomes true 4-wheeling. You might notice the lone grave beside the trail. Vandals have damaged it in recent years.

The lake is about 11,600 feet of Colorado High and is a beautiful place to picnic. Please use the existing trail. The grass at that elevation is very fragile.

When you return to Romley, continue up the railway toward the ghost town of Hancock. There is very little left of Hancock, however, other interesting buildings along the way will capture your interest.

Colorado's version of Italy's leaning tower is a well-known landmark among 4-wheelers.

A little mining camp tucked into the hillside behind it is well worth looking over. The cute little shack pictured is not as well preserved as it first appears. The whole back wall is caved in by a huge boulder that is almost big enough to fill it up. That would have been a rude awakening at 3 a.m. in the morning. I hope the poor miner who lived there was somewhere else when the rock announced its arrival.

As we wandered through the many buildings in the area, we could not help but wonder what stories each one was harboring.

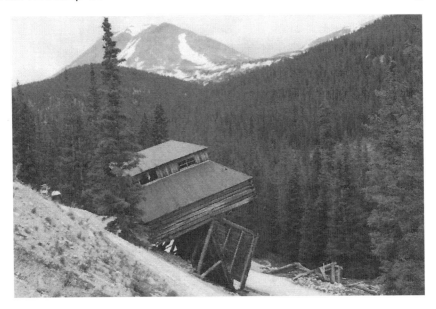

Stories about newlyweds with dreams of a brighter future. Shattered dreams that are still buried in the Mary Murphy Mine.

Stories about parties that lasted all night long or about arguments that were settled in blood. Whatever those stories might be, they shall remain untold, locked inside these crumbling walls ...

until some day, the walls come tumbling down ... and then the stories will be no more. The last witnesses to the tales of Romley's past will be gone forever.

There is a lot to see and do along the way to Romley and the Mary Murphy Mine. The fun begins in St. Elmo, a town that was once the most active city in the area. Pictures of it can be found in every ghost town book ever written even though it has never been a REAL ghost town. There have always been residents in St. Elmo.

In recent years, summer homes have begun springing up all around St. Elmo and many of the original buildings have been repaired to accommodate overnight occupants. After sitting idle for more than twenty years, St. Elmo lives again.

In its prime, St. Elmo was a party town ... the place to go on Saturday night. Miners from nearby communities and construction workers from the Alpine Tunnel all headed for St. Elmo to spend their earnings.

It was originally established with the name, Forest City, however, the post office refused to use that name due to a concern it would be confused with Forest City in California. They had visions of mail being delivered a thousand miles from where it was intended to go. (I guess that was unusual back in those days.) When the post office adopted the name of St. Elmo, the city began using it too.

Although its primary purpose was to serve as supply point for the miners and construction workers, St. Elmo was also the starting point for stage lines to Gunnison, Aspen, and Tin Cup. It claimed 1500 residents during its boom and had five hotels among its many businesses. There are rumors that one of the buildings is haunted by a woman who can sometimes be seen standing at an upstairs window.

GETTING LOST IN STYLE

The easiest map to use for the area is the San Isabel National Forest Map. On the other hand, the USGS Chaffe County maps show more detail.

HANCOCK PASS NAVIGATION

MARY MURPHY MINE, ROMLEY, & HANCOCK PASS

*The following odometer readings were taken using a '97 Isuzu Trooper.
The GPS positions were acquired by referencing Google Maps.*

ODO	Latitude N	Longitude W	Landmarks and descriptions
0.0	38.705932	106.340015	Turn off St. Elmo Road and onto Hancock Pass Road. Chaffe County 295
0.5	38 702375	106.346558	Continue straight. The road on the left goes to Iron Chest Mine.
2.9/0	38.673188	106.366721	This is Romley. The main road continues to Hancock. The road going left is for the Mary Murphy Mine and Pomeroy Lake. Reset trip meter to zero.
2.5/0	38.639438	106.361673	Hancock town site. Turn left for Hancock Pass. Reset trip meter. Straight is a hiking trail to the Alpine Tunnel.
0.2	38.638202	106.361336	Right turn on 299. Straight goes to Hancock Lake.
2.2	38 620890	106 374735	This is Hancock Pass.
3.6	38.611434	106.378544	Stay right. Left goes to Tomichi Pass.
4.2/0	38.613669	106.390009	Stay left onto Alpine Tunnel Road at Sherrod Loop. The road to the right goes to the Alpine Tunnel. Reset trip meter to zero.
1.0	38.625325	106.399065	Water Tank.
4.3	38.612263	106.450375	Midway Tank.
7.6	38 624999	106.475966	Right onto road for Cumberland Pass. Left goes 2.9 miles to Pitkin.

GENERAL AREA MAP

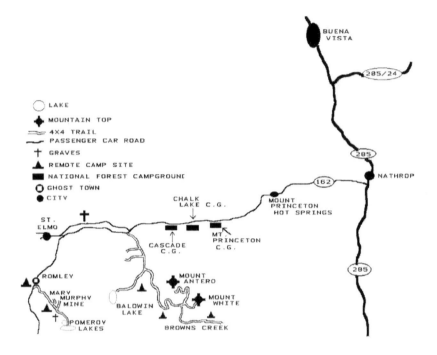

MT ANTERO

14,269 FEET IN ELEVATION

It is 14,269 feet to the peak of Mt. Antero and you can get your 4x4 within a few hundred feet of the peak. That's if you really have the desire to park your vehicle at an elevation normally reserved for airplanes. The number of places in the USA where you can do that, can be counted on your fingers. When you're on top of Mt. Antero, you're on top of the USA ... at least the part of it that is accessible in a vehicle.

We don't even count Pike's Peak because they charge so much to drive on it. The only reason a true 4-wheeler would even pay that price is just so he can say he has been there.

Parked at the top of Mt. Antero

When a tourist asks us about mountains, the conversation usually goes something like this.

Tourist: "Have you ever been to the top of Pike's Peak? Wow!"

4-wheeler: "Oh yeah. I been there. That's nothing compared to Mount Antero."

"Really?"

"Yeah, but it scares the socks off most flatlanders."

"Wow!" A pause while it soaks in. "Why?"

"It's them switchbacks. They make Black Bear Road look like a two-lane highway."

"Yeah, I heard of Black Bear. That's the one C. W. McCall wrote a song about. Antero's worse, huh?"

"No! It's better!" the 4-wheeler says with a smile. "But if you're not into driving switchbacks, while driving within inches away from a thousand-foot drop, you won't like it."

"Wow!"

"Yeah ... and at the switchbacks ... you wouldn't believe it ... no vehicle can turn sharp enough to turn them in one pass ... and while you're turning, you're climbing ... kicking rocks over the edge that seem to fall forever."

"Sounds outta sight!"

"Not at all. In fact, when you get to the top, everything is in sight for hundreds of miles. You can just sit in your 4x4 and look down on the whole state. I like to turn off the engine and just listen."

"Listen to what?"

"That's the point. There's nothing to listen to. It's the most peaceful place in the entire world."

"Majestic!"

"Yeah, but then you gotta go back down. Try to imagine going down a steep mountainside that makes a sharp turn on the way down ... so sharp, you have to pull around until your wheels are near the edge of the cliff ... then you have to hold your vehicle in that position (pointing downhill and hanging on the edge) while you shift into reverse so you can back up and finish the turn."

"No thanks!"

"Well, like I said, Mount Antero scares the socks off some flatlanders.

And so, Mount Antero belongs to those who dare tread where eagles never go. There are two distinct levels along the journey. Some folks turn around before they ever get to the first level. It comes at the top of the switchbacks pictured here. At that point the road forks in several directions. The left fork continues to the second level of Mt. Antero. The middle fork goes up the side of Mount White but not quite to its 13,667-foot peak. The right fork leads to a forested area along Browns Creek. I am told the fishing is great in the lake.

Getting to the lake from the peak is very easy. Just follow the path across the open valley all the way down into the forest. There are spots where the trail is nearly grown over by brush so be prepared for brush marks in your paint. Normally referred to as Colorado Pin Striping.

Some places are rocky, but easily maneuvered. There are excellent camping spots all through the forest, many of them beside the creek. The mosquitoes in that area are very fat. That's because we feed'um tourists. If you want a few for souvenirs, you're welcome to take as many of them home with you as you like.

While you're going across that open valley toward the creek, you'll pass an old cabin and a mine that was still open the last time we checked. The entrance to the mine is so small, you must crawl on your stomach to get in, but once inside, there is plenty of room to stand up.

This mine has timbers so it does not pass our test for entrance. We do not enter any mine unless it's cut from solid rock. The second mark against it is the small entrance. Such mines can have bad air. If you enter a mine with bad air, you will never know it. You simply go to sleep ... for good.

I watched some people go in and waited for them to come out. I asked them how it was and they replied, "Spooky Timbers!" We advise you to pass this one up.

The trail to the second level on Mount Antero is really nasty. If the first switchbacks worried you, stay off the second level. A rookie could get into serious trouble in a heartbeat on that section. That level normally has snow on it until mid-August. In some years, we have been able to get to the first level in July.

The air at 14,000 ft. is a little thin. Those of you from out of state should spend a few days at lower elevations before tackling this one. If you feel dizzy, nauseous, or get a headache, don't assume it was that bologna sandwich you had for lunch. It could be altitude sickness. Get back down below tree line as fast as you can safely do so.

There is a side trail at the creek crossing where the NFS sign explains the rules of the road. It follows the creek to Baldwin Lake, then to the mine pictured. The trail is rough, rocky, and often muddy. It ends in a basin and does not offer the scenic views available on Mt. Antero.

NAVIGATION FOR MT ANTERO

Mt. Antero is south and west of Nathrop, Colorado. Go south of town and turn right on the road marked as Chaffe County 162. The paved road will take you to Mt. Princeton Hot Springs Lodge. The Mt. Antero road is located between Mt. Princeton Hot Springs and St. Elmo. It is 7.8 miles from Mt. Princeton and 3.4 miles from St. Elmo.			
The following odometer readings were taken using a '97 Isuzu Trooper. The GPS positions were taken using a Magellan GPS4000 XL			
ODO	**Latitude N**	**Longitude W**	**Landmarks and descriptions**
0.0	38 42.6012	106 17.4984	**Turn at the sign for Mt. Antero and shift to 4-Lo. Reset trip meter.**
2.6	38 40.9540	106 16.3673	**Left for Mt Antero. Right goes to Baldwin Lake.**
5.9	38 39.7071	106 15.4779	**First Level. 13,119 feet**
7.2	38 40.0420	106 14.9730	**Level Two. 13,784 ft. It's a long walk to the peak from here.**

GETTING LOST IN STYLE

The San Isabel National Forest map has the entire area on it. For more detail, get the USGS Chaffe County maps number 2 & 3.

SAN JUAN MOUNTAIN AREA

Until a decade or so ago, the reputation of the 4x4 trails in the San Juan's were enough to keep many people away. Their names were whispered around campfires ... like the names of the gunslingers who once lived in their midst.

"Bat Masterson ... Butch Cassidy ... Kid Curry."

"Black Bear Road ... Engineer Pass ... Imogene Pass."

"Yeah, I heard of'um," one 4-wheeler would say. "We gotta go there some day," another would comment. "Yeah ... maybe someday."

The days of such reputations have come and gone. Just as the gunslingers faded into history, so did most of the danger that surrounded the trails. That's not to say you can't get into trouble in the San Juan's. There are still many trails that have been wiped out by rock slides or avalanches and attempting to tackle them in a vehicle could be fatal, but it is not necessary to travel those trails to get through the area.

Most of the main trails, like Engineer Pass and Cinnamon Pass are dug out in June to allow passage of the rental 4X4s available in Ouray, Silverton, and Lake City. If you go that early in the year, you may be traveling through narrow snow canals with walls of snow twenty feet high on both sides. Water on the floor of those snow canals can be two-feet deep in places and the muddy surface beneath the water can be very slippery.

By the time the fourth of July rolls around, the snow and water on the graded roads is normally gone. Other roads, like Black Bear and Poughkeepsie Gulch may still be closed or impassable until August.

If you are unfamiliar with the term, "Shelf Road", the San Juan's will define it for you in a way you will never forget. A good example is the short stretch between Highway 550 and Poughkeepsie Gulch where the trail is cut out of a sheer vertical cliff. Although it is plenty wide for a full-size vehicle, some folks would rather walk than drive.

One such road is the descent into Telluride on Black Bear Road.

The drop-off is not as sheer, but in some places a full-size vehicle's tires are close enough to the edge to kick rocks over the side. The switchbacks are extremely tight and cannot be negotiated in one try. From inside the vehicle, the front-end seems to be hanging out over nothing but air as you pull forward to the cliff's edge, then back up enough to make a second try. Passengers find themselves pushing on imaginary brakes and spotters will yell, "Whoa!" long before it's time. The danger is so obvious that it is not dangerous at all. The only way we could imagine getting hurt on Black Bear is to do something really stupid ... like putting the vehicle in a forward gear instead of reverse, forgetting to set the emergency brake (Never trust "P" on your automatic to hold the vehicle), or driving too close to the edge. Inexperienced drivers should always have a spotter (someone outside the vehicle) to be sure the path chosen is the right one.

The reputations of the trails in the San Juan's still live, as do the reputations of old gunslingers, but reality is far different. In fact, your odds of getting in trouble are much greater if you drive I-25 through Denver during rush hour than to drive the San Juan Trails in this book.

On the other hand, the scenic marvels of the San Juan's are impossible to describe. For that reason, nothing you hear or see in pictures will come close to the experience of standing in their midst. "Little Switzerland", as it is called, is some of Colorado's most magnificent scenic wonder.

Historic interest is as much a part of the San Juan experience as being there. Ghost towns, old mines, tramways, stagecoach stops, and deserted cabins all have stories to tell. Some of those stories are repeated in this book and other books for sale in the three major towns, but others are for your imagination to discover.

Some abandoned mines in the area are still open. Entering them is extremely dangerous, but if you intend to risk your life to explore them, bring big lights. We use the small spotlights that are designed to plug into the vehicle cigarette lighter. We plug it into a portable 12-volt battery pack which can be recharged in the vehicle cigarette lighter. Once you light these old relics up, you see colors and minerals that were probably never even seen by the original miners. We have our own set of rules for determining if we will enter a mine. Those rules are NOT based on knowledge ... just fear.

(1) We never enter a mine that has wooden supports. If the miners had doubts about the stability of the ceiling a century ago, we won't get close to it. Many of those supports are over 100 years old and rotten.

(2) Never touch the walls or ceiling. They might come down around you.

(3) Never walk in water deeper than the light can penetrate. That little water puddle in the floor could be the top of a bottomless vertical shaft.

(4) Unless you are sure of the mines stability ... no loud noises.

(5) Check for bear tracks before going in.

We don't say our list is a good one. Nor do we claim it is a good one. Nor do we suggest you use it. Entering an old mine is dangerous and can be fatal. If you don't feel safe going in ... don't go. You just might be psychic.

A mine can kill you silently if it has bad air. You simply go to sleep.

This is the left side of a two-page map.

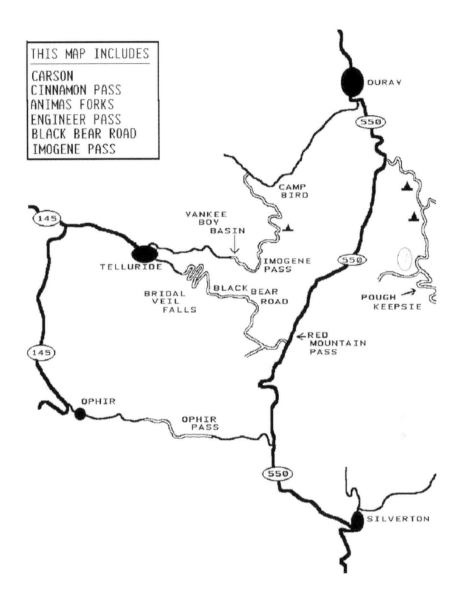

THIS MAP INCLUDES

CARSON
CINNAMON PASS
ANIMAS FORKS
ENGINEER PASS
BLACK BEAR ROAD
IMOGENE PASS

DURAY

550

CAMP
BIRD

VANKEE
BOY
BASIN

145

TELLURIDE

IMOGENE
PASS

550

POUGH →
KEEPSIE

BLACK BEAR
ROAD

BRIDAL
VEIL
FALLS

145

OPHIR

OPHIR
PASS

← RED
MOUNTAIN
PASS

550

SILVERTON

This is the right side of a two-page map.

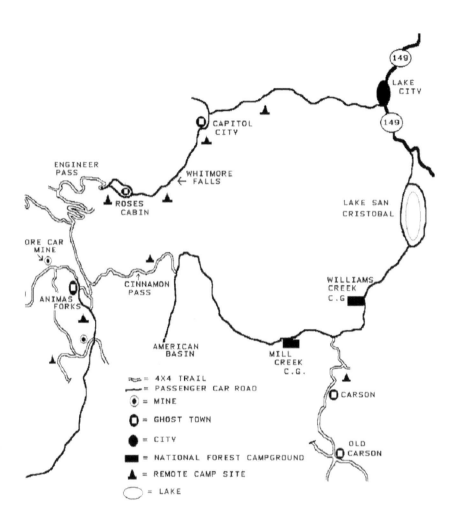

149

LAKE
CITY

149

CAPITOL
CITY

ENGINEER
PASS

WHITMORE
← FALLS

LAKE SAN
CRISTOBAL

ROSES
CABIN

ORE CAR
MINE

CINNAMON
PASS

WILLIAMS
CREEK
C.G

ANIMAS
FORKS

AMERICAN
BASIN

MILL
CREEK
C.G.

CARSON

OLD
CARSON

≈ = 4X4 TRAIL

——— = PASSENGER CAR ROAD

⦿ = MINE

⬯ = GHOST TOWN

⬤ = CITY

▬ = NATIONAL FOREST CAMPGROUND

▲ = REMOTE CAMP SITE

⬭ = LAKE

CARSON GHOST TOWN AND WAGER GULCH

"Breaker 13 for the Shotgun. Outlaw lookin' fer-ya. Kick it back."

"10-4 Outlaw. We're bringin' up the backdoor with Bandit, Bad Brad, and Santa Anna in the Rockin' Chair. Kick it back?"

"10-4 Shotgun. Everything in Lake City is closed for the night. When you get to town, make a right turn on 2nd street and follow the signs for Engineer Pass. Mercy sakes alive. Looks like we gotta Pass Patrol!"

Capitol City Camp

We were getting in late after spending the past three days checking out Mount Antero, Romley, Mary Murphy, & Tincup. So far, our Fourth of July week had been super. Warm days, cold nights, and lots of Colorado blue skies. We were headed for one of Pass Patrol's favorite group camping spots at the site of the ghost town of Capitol City.

It is a beautiful, huge, campsite on the banks of Henson Creek. Sheep herders use the corral and have built a pit toilet that remains open to the public. It is also accessible to motor homes or, in our case, a trailer carrying a Jeep. A beautiful place for a San Juan base camp.

(In recent years, we have abandoned this site in favor of others. Notice the single tent in the previous photo.)

The guys set up the tents while the kids built a fire and the gals dug out the vittles. It's amazing how fast all that can happen when everyone is tired and hungry.

Capitol City was so named because its founder thought it would become the capitol of Colorado. Apparently, his imagination far exceeded reality. There is nothing left of the original mining town. Summer homes and cabins are being built in the area. Most of the privately-owned lots are fenced off.

Lake City, CO

When the morning sun peeked over the canyon wall, it found us all still asleep. By the time 9 a.m. rolled around, a few of us crawled out of our sleeping bags and somebody sparked a fire. This was our fourth day of 4-wheeling and we were eager to get it started.

"Shucks, we even got outta camp before 10 a.m. Well, almost before 10 a.m." We were in a kick-back, have a good time, smell the roses, stick the toes in the water, & toss a rock off the edge, kinda mood. We headed back to Lake City for fuel and supplies. Everything we needed was available in Lake City. The decision was made to follow a loop through Carson, Cinnamon Pass, Animas Forks, Engineer Pass, and back to camp. We headed south out of Lake City about two miles and turned right at the sign for Cinnamon Pass & Lake San Cristobal.

There are two major National Forest Campgrounds on that road. Both require reservations during busy times of the year. One is called the Williams Creek C.G. and the other is called the Mill Creek C.G. Between those two campgrounds is a sign pointing up Wager Gulch with "Carson" printed on it.

Carson was actually two separate communities. The older one was on the opposite side of the Continental Divide from the one at a lower elevation. Older books that have not been updated describe the infamous trail to Carson as one of the worst in the state ... but that's just another gunslinger story.

In fact, during late summer, a high clearance 2x4 could make it all the way to the new town site and maybe even all the way to the divide. The buildings in New Carson are still in abnormally good condition, complete with roofs. In this picture, you can see New Carson in the trees from the trail leading to Old Carson.

A walk-through Carson is a walk into the past. The way the buildings are grouped indicates how much they depended on each, other to survive. Tightly grouped.

Turn your imagination loose and help the old town come back to life. Focus on where you are. Imagine it buzzing with mining activity, mules loaded with silver or gold, women washing clothes in the creek, nurses bandaging injured miners in the boarding house, and children chasing each other around the buildings. Carson was a busy place. Can you feel it? Can you feel the energy they left behind?

Our next stop was Old Carson. You can still find logs and other remains of the original site by following the trail past New Carson to the Great Divide. There are probably lots of reasons why it was moved, but none were recorded. One of the stories being passed around is because old Carson was built on top of an iron ore deposit. In other words, it was built upon a natural lightning rod. Since lightning is a common occurrence at that altitude, Carson may have been moved because its residents were getting tired of having their homes fried.

Remains of Old Carson

This photo shows the single building left standing at Old Carson. The vehicle in the distance is coming from New Carson

The road beyond Old Carson continues Southeast to Heart Lake.

From Old Carson, we headed back down Wager Gulch to the road over Cinnamon Pass. With all the road work that has been done in recent years, the trip to the pass has been done in a passenger car, but low clearance vehicles are not recommended.

Cinnamon Pass climbs to 12,640 ft. before beginning its journey down to Animas Forks.

Cinnamon Pass began as a wagon road for the same purpose we used it for on our trip ... to get between Lake City and Animas Forks.

CARSON GHOST TOWN NAVIGATION

The following odometer readings were taken using a '97 Isuzu Trooper.
The GPS positions were acquired referencing Google Maps.

Lake City to Carson ghost town			
ODO	Latitude N	Longitude W	Landmarks and descriptions
0.0	38.026066	107.317320	Bridge on south side of town.
2.2	38.000385	107.298854	Right at sign for Lake San Cristobal.
8.9	37.921570	107.332882	Williams Creek Campground.
10.3	37.907985	107.345361	Castle Lakes Campground.
11.1/0	37.905967	107.360456	Left goes up Wager Gulch to Carson. Reset meter. Watch closely for private property signs and take the roads that are open.
3.4/0 approx.	37.869126	107.362338	New Carson. Reset meter when you get back to main road.
1.4 approx.	37.856406	107.367962	The exact location of Upper Carson (Old Carson) is difficult to pinpoint. There are some old buildings scattered around the area.

GETTING LOST IN STYLE

The Gunnison National Forest Map contains most of the San Juan area listed in this book. The USGS county maps are also very handy. Carson is in Hinsdale County.

ANIMAS FORKS GHOST TOWN AND CALIFORNIA GULCH

Animas Forks, with California Gulch in the background, is impressive, especially from the shelf road above it. Some of the abandoned buildings still retain their roofs.

A common tale, true or not, is a local judge once told a lawyer that he could not take his case to a higher court. His court, far above timberline, was the highest court in the country.

Snow depth in this small town did, and still does, often exceed 20 feet. Even in the summer, temperatures can dip below freezing. Staying alive in Animas Forks must have been a full-time job.

Even so, it was a busy community. Besides telephone service connected to Lake City over Engineer Pass, Animas Forks served as a rail head for a line to Eureka. Keeping those rails clear of snow was an extremely dangerous task. Avalanches often wiped out the rails as well as those who were trying to keep them open.

At one time, Animas Forks claimed a population of 1000 folks, but most of them left for the winter. One winter they left and never came back.

Another interesting tale often passed around concerns a newspaper called the Animas Forks Pioneer. Apparently, a law existed stating that mining patent notices had to appear in a newspaper, so an enterprising fella started one for the miners to use. It instantly became required reading for anyone in the mining business and the first issue sold for $500. That first issue probably covered his initial investment, but the Pioneer thrived for long after that with an average price of about $25 per copy. When the claims played out and the Pioneer was no longer needed, its owner probably took his money and retired ... to a warmer climate.

Animas Forks

Unlike many of the ghost towns in Colorado, Animas Forks was built to stay. In other words, it consisted of real buildings instead of tents.

As you wander through them, notice how sturdy they were built. Consider they have continued to stand after being abandoned for over seventy years. They have managed to withstand snow, hail, wind, lightening, and even the most destructive force on earth ... people. But time is taking its toll. The walls are crumbling, the floors are broken through, and vandalism is evident in all the buildings.

We have used them on several occasions for noon time shelter, but there are too many rodents to use them at night. We prefer to set up our tents alongside the creek.

One house draws more attention than the others because of its huge bay window. Apparently, the house was occupied by a wealthy mine owner named Welsh. According to several references, his daughter was the owner of the famous Hope

Diamond which was purchased with Colorado gold. She later authored a book titled, "Father Struck It Rich" which can still be found in local book stores.

Regardless of what secrets this house will take to its demise, the fact is, it is a real eye-catcher. The stairway to its second level is still in place, but not exactly safe. Better to admire from a distance. There are also some foundations from the huge mill that was once the center of activity for the small town.

There are lots of old mines to explore in the area. Our favorite is the one with the ore cars in California Gulch. It is located just past the intersection for Placer Gulch. Unfortunately, vandals have destroyed one of the ore cars in the mine by dragging it out.

PLEASE DON'T DAMAGE ANY OF COLORADO'S HISTORIC RELICS. BECAUSE OF ONE THOUGHTLESS ACT, OUR CHILDREN CAN NEVER SEE THIS RELIC AS IT ONCE WAS. IF YOU SEE SOMEONE DAMAGING SOMETHING, REPORT THEM TO THE FOREST SERVICE. DO NOT CONFRONT THEM DIRECTLY, BUT TAKE PHOTOS OF THE ACT FOR EVIDENCE IF POSSIBLE.

A second ore car is still in the mine and sits under a chute that connects the upper level mine to the one the ore cars are in. Apparently, the two mines had only one set of rails. The ore was tossed into the chute from above, fell into the car below, and was hauled out the entrance.

(Due to the act of two thoughtless vandals, this ore car no longer exists in the location pictured.)

The mine is cut from solid rock and meets our standards for entry as outlined earlier. Remember, we are not qualified to determine if a mine is safe to enter. You enter these old relics at your own risk so don't go if you don't feel safe doing so. You just might be psychic.

Unlike many old mines, this one has very little water in it. Although you may get your feet wet, your ankles should stay dry.

Although our battery powered spotlight and our camera flash did a decent job of lighting the mine, there is total darkness waiting for you. If your flashlight dies, you will see what that means. Best take two.

We were amazed at the variety of colors our camera found in the mine. Nearly every color in the rainbow. The battery pack and spot light mentioned earlier is a real bonus for exploring this one.

GETTING LOST IN STYLE

The Uncompahgre National Forest Map includes Animas Forks, Silverton, and California Gulch. The USGS San Juan County Topo Map can also be used.

Note: The GPS positions in the following table were acquired by referencing Google Maps. The readings found in the original stories were determined to be unreliable.

ANIMAS FORKS NAVIGATION

The following odometer readings were taken using a '97 Isuzu Trooper.
The GPS positions were acquired by referencing Google Maps.

ODO	Latitude N	Longitude W	Landmarks and descriptions
The following navigation picks up where the Carson Ghost Town Navigation left off. It begins at the point where the Wager Gulch Road sign points to Carson.			
0.0	37.905967	107.360456	This is on the Cinnamon Pass Road at the point where Wager Gulch (Hinsdale County 36) goes to Carson.
1.2	37.907104	107.381412	Public Outhouse
1.8	37.907337	107.392816	Mill Creek Campground
3.0/0	37.903748	107.411865	Right fork. The ghost town of Sherman is 0.8 miles to the left on Hinsdale County 35. Reset your trip meter.
4.1	37.936970	107.460839	Burrows Park. Public Outhouse.
7.7	37.931219	107.514331	Right fork. American Basin is left.
8.2	37.935398	107.515031	Tabasco Mill
9.9	37.933704	107.538116	Cinnamon Pass 12,640 feet.
12.0	37.933863	107.568637	Left at T intersection above Animas Forks. A right turn will take you to Engineer Pass.
12.3	37.929907	107.565662	The switchback to the right goes to Animas Forks. Left is a shortcut to Silverton.
12.7	37.929842	107.569431	Animas Forks Public outhouse is next to the jail.

ENGINEER PASS

12,800 FEET IN ELEVATION

"Breaker 13. Hey Outlaw. The girls wanna know how far we gotta go on this shelf road. They don't like it."

That is not an uncommon reaction to the west side of the Engineer Pass road. It is not extremely narrow, but there is a vertical wall on one side and a vertical cliff on the other. In other words, "It scares the whatsit outta some folks."

We had left Animas Forks and headed north to the intersection of Engineer Pass and Ouray. The sun was nearly gone for the day and the only daylight left was at the top of the mountains. Our camp was on the other side of the pass and some of us were looking forward to doing a little moonlighting. (That's Pass Patrol's definition for night time 4-wheeling.)

"Just tell'um to close their eyes and it'll be okay."

"10-4." After a pause. "Nope. That ain't workin' either," Santa Anna giggled.

Imagine a cloudless star-filled sky where every formation appeared crystal clear. Imagine turning off the vehicle and looking out over hundreds of miles of mountain peaks in a country so remote that not one man-made light could be seen in any direction. Oh yes. Such a moment is unforgettably inspiring.

We spent several minutes on the summit before going down the east side toward Lake City. Bandit lit up the road with his Warn off-road lights. That night, campfire talk centered around the ghost towns and, of course, the gals dislike of Engineer Pass.

"Well," I groaned as I raised up off the log where I had been sitting. "Guess I better get some shut-eye. We gotta go back over Engineer Pass tomorrow to get to Black Bear Road."

"What!" It sounded like practice for a chorus show.

When morning came, we hurried as fast as we could go to get started. "Shucks. We musta got outta camp by 10 a.m. Well, almost 10 a.m."

Our first stop was Whitmore Falls. This was early spring, Fourth of July Weekend, and the water was raging over it. The roar was so loud, we had to use hand signals to communicate.

Whitmore Falls

Getting back out of the canyon where Whitmore Falls resides is a very long and steep climb.

The water is snow-melt-cold and moving fast.

A little farther up the road is a roadside toilet and camp site, then the location of Rose's Cabin. Mr. Rose was an enterprising fella. He constructed his way-station along the path between Lake City and the mining camps to take advantage of the traffic going in both directions. Stagecoach teams were quickly changed while the drivers and passengers took advantage of the bar and gambling inside. There were over twenty rooms upstairs for anyone wishing to spend the night and a safe was available to store valuables.

Rose's Cabin Site

Remains of old safe

Such activity was routine for Rose's Cabin. It was the main stage stop between Silverton and Lake City. The old safe still lies in the meadow but vandals have chosen to shoot it full of holes. Another remnant from the past is needlessly destroyed.

You can bet the trail over Engineer Pass in a stage coach was a nerve-shaking, bone-rattling, experience that the passenger would never forget.

"I'll never forget it either," Connie remarked as we headed down the west side toward Silverton.

"Don't worry gals," I answered. "We only have to cross it two or three more times." There are times when I am so glad I am way ahead of the other vehicles. It's hard to throw a rock that far.

"Don't go feelin' too safe, Outlaw," Connie teased. "This trail has a switchback coming up and we'll be above you."

"Aw-oh! ... I was just kidding gals. I'll bring you back another way."

By the time we got down, they decided Engineer wasn't nearly so bad in the day light. Especially after I explained that the only way around was 150 miles of highway instead of 10 miles of trail.

Unfortunately, Black Bear was still closed on the Fourth of July. We ended up doing some shopping in Silverton and Ouray which got the gals in a good mood for the trip back to camp. The only bad part was they were having too much fun and shopped a little too long. We didn't leave Ouray until dark and we still had to get over Engineer Pass. "Oh well, this time I'll be on top at the switchbacks."

It was a great trip, and the latest cards I got from Illinois says they wanna go again. And the one thing they insist we do at least once, is to go over Engineer after dark ... just for ole time's sake.

ADDED UPDATE

In loving memory of Reggie and Connie (Shotgun). Both were killed in an auto accident a few years after this trip near their home in Nason, Illinois. I knew them both from the days when we were children in a one-room school house.

GETTING LOST IN STYLE

If you would like to have some extra maps of the area, the Uncompahgre National Forest Service Map is a good one. If you prefer USGS county topo maps, the Engineer Pass Road between Lake City and Ouray crosses parts of Hinsdale County, San Juan County, and Ouray County. All the roads in the area are well marked to benefit the Jeep-rental companies. They send tourists over them daily in rented vehicles so they make sure there is not much danger of getting lost or damaging anything. As time goes on, all the roads in the area are becoming more like graded county roads eliminating the need for 4-wheel drive, but the scenery still makes it one of our favorite places.

NAVIGATION FOR ENGINEER PASS

ODO	Latitude N	Longitude W	Landmarks and descriptions
The following odometer readings were taken using a '97 Isuzu Trooper. *The GPS positions were acquired by referencing Google Maps.*			
0.0			Leave Ouray at the sign that says Silverton is 23 miles.
2.3			Pass through a tunnel and arrive at the Bear Creek water fall.
3.5/0	37.988604	107.649584	Turn off for Engineer Pass Road. Reset trip meter.
1.6	37.975077	107.635499	Mickey Breene Mine.
2.0	37.970376	107.630840	Turnoff for the Killer Rabbit Camp.
2.4	37.967009	107.627257	Left at intersection for Poughkeepsie Gulch.
4.2	37.965501	107.608676	Sawmill and the Des Ouray Mine.
5.8	37.963217	107.592324	Public Outhouse.
7.0	37.957404	107.575514	Turn left for Engineer Pass. Straight goes to Animas Forks and on to Silverton.

SAN JUAN TOUR DAY ONE

There is so much to see and do in the San Juan's, it's difficult for a first timer to get much of it covered due to distractions. We believe the best way is to have a pre-set auto tour with every stop and attraction marked along the way. The following pages include just such a tour. We hope it will be helpful to you in making the most of your time.

The first objective is deciding where to start. This tour begins in Lake City. From Denver, that is about a six-hour drive.

Trip Meter	LANDMARKS AND AREA DESCRIPTIONS.
0.0	In Lake City, turn west on 2nd street and reset your meter to zero.
9.1	This is Capitol City. Turn left at the main intersection. There are magnificent views of the creek and Canyon along the way but be aware and respect private property. Capitol City is mostly private summer homes.
9.3	A dirt trail goes across a meadow on the left. We used this as a campsite in the past and may still be available but progress is closing in on it fast. An outhouse and corral marks the location.
10.9	Whitmore Falls. The short hike out to the overlook or down to the creek is strenuous.
14.3	Road side rest room and camp site. From this point the road is rated as Easy/Scary. Roses Cabin is a short distance away.

ODO	Latitude N	Longitude W	Landmarks and descriptions
14.4/0.0	37.976359	107.538080	Roses Cabin. Reset trip meter.

Rose's Cabin is long gone, however, parts of the stable, iron safe, and corrals were still there in '98. There are numerous campsites in the valley behind the cabin site. There is also a road at the far end of the valley going up the mountain to the Galconda Mine. The building at the Galconda Mine is very similar in size and shape to the original Rose's Cabin. Turn right at the junction just before getting to the cabin for the Engineer Pass Road. Reset your trip meter.

Note: Our trip mileage readings may differ from yours depending on tire size, tire pressure, and individual vehicle odometer accuracy. For that reason, we will frequently reset to zero in an effort to keep the variances lower.

Note: If you decide to look for the Galconda Mine, follow the road behind Rose's Cabin. Most of the intersections go to campsites, however, one of them crosses the creek. The one going across the creek is the one that goes to the Galconda Mine. This is not the one with the bridge.

NAVIGATION FOR SAN JUAN TOUR CONTINUED

Trip Meter	LANDMARKS AND AREA DESCRIPTIONS.
0.0	Leave the intersection at Rose's Cabin going uphill and west crossing Engineer Pass.
5.5	Intersection. Yvonne Pass is left. Turn right to continue the tour. A side trip off the Yvonne Pass road was a way to drive to the peak of Engineer Mountain but it has been closed. Another foot trail from the top of Yvonne Pass can be used to hike to Rose's Cabin. It is also possible to see the Galconda Mine from the peak of Yvonne Pass.
6.5	The next intersection has a sign pointing left for Animas Forks and right for Ouray. This tour goes to Animas Forks. Turn left.

8.9	On the way to Animas Forks, you will pass the intersection going uphill for Cinnamon Pass. At that point, you can see Animas Forks on your right. Continue downhill and arrive at Animas Forks. Many of the buildings are falling down.

Leave Animas Forks going south past the pit toilet and across the creek toward Silverton. At 1.3 miles from Animas Forks, you will arrive at another intersection. Picayne (also spelled Picayune) is on the right. Burns Gulch is across the creek on the left. Remember this spot for Day Two of the tour. Continue toward Silverton.

The site of where Eureka used to be is now a camping area. The tour for Day One stops here. Day Two begins here.

There are other campsites between Eureka and Silverton. Silverton has motels, hotels, and a campground. Fuel and supplies of all kinds are available. We recommend dinner at the Grand Imperial Hotel and camping at the Eureka ghost town site.

SAN JUAN TOUR DAY TWO

Trip Meter	LANDMARKS AND AREA DESCRIPTIONS.
0.0	Leave Eureka. Reset your trip meter at the bridge.
2.8	Go toward Animas Forks and stop at the intersection for Picayune Gulch and Burns Gulch. The trail up Burns Gulch begins by crossing the creek. There is another access to it a short distance further at the bridge. It is two miles to the basin at the top where a mine and storage room can be found. It is a scenic trip but is rated as difficult near the top.

The following side trip turns up Picayune Gulch. This section is rated as Easy/Scary.

ODO	Latitude N	Longitude W	Landmarks and descriptions
0.0	37.916380	107.558084	Reset the trip meter to zero. The first part of this trip can be Scary, especially if you have to pass a vehicle coming the other way.
0.2			There is an open mine alongside the road, however, to visit requires driving all the way to the top and hiking down. We use a spotlight and portable battery pack for mines.

Note: Entering old mines is dangerous. We are not qualified to determine which ones are safe to enter. Use your own judgment.

Trip Meter	LANDMARKS AND AREA DESCRIPTIONS.
0.4	At the next intersection, turn right to go to Placer Gulch.
1.3	You will pass the Treasure Mountain Mine. Several interesting buildings are still standing.
3.4	Stay right at the intersection for Parson Lake. The road continues upward.

Respect private property as posted.

Trip Meter	LANDMARKS AND AREA DESCRIPTIONS.
4.7	The road rides the ridge for a while, then begins descending some narrow switchbacks into Placer Gulch. These are rated as Easy/Scary. The Gold Prince Mine at the bottom of the Switchbacks once delivered its ore to the Gold Prince Mill in Animas Forks by way of a tram. Many of the supports for the tram are still visible. The mine was operated as an extension of the Sunnyside Mine in later years.

ODO	Latitude N	Longitude W	Landmarks and descriptions
6.4/0	37.931751	107.589830	The Placer Gulch Road connects to the California Gulch road at this point. Turn left and reset meter.
2.7	This is California Pass. 12,930ft.		

Trip Meter	LANDMARKS AND AREA DESCRIPTIONS.
3.1	The road descends into Poughkeepsie Gulch. Left at the intersection.
3.8/0	Hurricane Pass. Reset the trip meter.
1.5	Take the right fork to Corkscrew Pass. Left goes to Silverton.

There is one intersection on the way up. Take the left fork.

ODO	Latitude N	Longitude W	Landmarks and descriptions
2.5	37.906579	107.660864	This is Corkscrew Pass. Continue over the top.
6.0	37.939259	107.671825	This is Highway 550. Turn right on the Highway for lunch in Ouray. The next section begins in Ouray.

Note: The ratings of the trails in this book are entirely the opinion of the author. You may see them differently depending on your experience and individual opinions.

The following table is an addition with the latest update and has a more consistent format. It has more information including more GPS positions. If you are following this tour, you should be finished with lunch by now and ready for a pleasant afternoon.

Ouray to Silverton by way of the Engineer Pass Road

ODO	Latitude N	Longitude W	Landmarks and descriptions
The following odometer readings were taken using a '97 Isuzu Trooper.			
The GPS positions were acquired by referencing Google Maps.			
0.0			Leave Ouray at the sign that says Silverton is 23 miles.
2.3			Pass through a tunnel and arrive at the Bear Creek water fall.
3.5/0	37.988604	107.649584	Turn off for Engineer Pass Road. Reset trip meter.
1.6	37.975077	107.635499	Mickey Breene Mine.
2.0	37.970376	107.630840	Turnoff for the Killer Rabbit Camp.
2.4	37.967009	107.627257	Left at intersection for Poughkeepsie Gulch.
4.2	37.965501	107.608676	Sawmill and the Des Ouray Mine.
4.4	37.964214	107.605572	Left at this intersection.
5.1	37.961934	107.595554	Left at Mineral Point Intersection.
The right fork goes to the San Juan Chief Mill over some rather difficult sections.			
5.8	37.963217	107.592324	Public Outhouse.
From this area, you can see the San Juan Chief Mill and buildings. The last intersection would have taken you to them. The next intersection will do so too.			
6.1	37.961412	107.586778	The road on the right goes to the San Juan Chief Mill.
7.0	37.957404	107.575514	Go straight to Animas Forks and on to Silverton.
8.9	37.933878	107.568625	Stay right at Cinnamon Pass Intersection
9.3	37.929861	107.565640	Take the left fork to Silverton. Right fork goes to Animas Forks.
9.5	37.926717	107.563192	Continue straight. Right goes to Animas Forks and an outhouse.

10.3	37.916380	107.558084	**You are back at Picayune Gulch and the end of Day 2.**

Note: There are lots of great camping spots along the road between Animas Forks and Silverton. Check out the area around Minnie Gulch and Maggie Gulch.

Day 3 begins in Eureka so we recommend camping there. Get lots of rest. Tomorrow will be a long day.

SAN JUAN TOUR
DAY THREE

DAY 3 – STONY PASS LOOP- PACK A LUNCH

Day 3 of the tour begins in Eureka. It will be a long day if you choose to do all of it. Be sure to pack a lunch.

NAVIGATION FOR DAY 3

The following odometer readings were taken using a '97 Isuzu Trooper. The GPS positions were acquired by referencing Google Maps.			
ODO	**Latitude N**	**Longitude W**	**Landmarks and descriptions**
0.0	37.879704	107.565735	Reset your meter at the bridge over the Animas River at Eureka.
2.7	37.916380	107.558084	You are back at Picayune Gulch Continue toward Cinnamon Pass.
3.5	37.926717	107.563192	Right Fork. Left goes to Animas Forks and an outhouse.
3.7	37.929861	107.565640	Take the right fork to Cinnamon Pass. The left fork goes to Animas Forks.
4.1/0	37.933878	107.568625	Turn right toward Cinnamon Pass. Left goes to Engineer Pass. Reset your trip meter.
2.1	37.933704	107.538116	Cinnamon Pass 12,640 feet.
3.8	37.935398	107.515031	Tabasco Mill
4.3	37.931219	107.514331	Left fork. American Basin is right.
7.9	37.936970	107.460839	Burrows Park. Public Outhouse.
12.0	37.903748	107.411865	Right fork. The ghost town of Sherman is 0.8 miles to the left on Hinsdale County 35. Reset your trip meter.

NAVIGATION FOR DAY 3 CONTINUED

ODO	Latitude N	Longitude W	Landmarks and descriptions
The following odometer readings were taken using a '97 Isuzu Trooper. The GPS positions were acquired by referencing Google Maps.			
13.2	37.907337	107.392816	Mill Creek Campground
13.8	37.907104	107.381412	Public Outhouse
15.0	37.905967	107.360456	Turn right onto the Wager Gulch Road (Hinsdale County 36). This road goes to the ghost towns of Carson.
3.4/0	37.869126	107.362338	This is New Carson. Reset meter when you get back to main road.
1.4	37.856406	107.367962	Take left fork. The exact location of Upper Carson (Old Carson) is difficult to pinpoint.
Unlike New Carson, Old Carson was apparently scattered. There are some old buildings scattered around the area.			
2.3	37.854383	107.350036	Left at sign for FSR 518.
4.6	37.833309	107.321434	Left at Heart Lake sign. Heart Lake is a dead-end road with a steep hike to lake. Nice campsites there.
5.7	37.836931	107.304350	Right. Stay on FSR 518.
7.2	37.820446	107.292333	Right. Stay on FSR 518.
8.8	37.814542	107.271296	Right on main gravel road. Pearl Lakes Trout Club is left.
9.3	37.808020	107.272300	Straight through intersection.
12.6	37.814274	107.221619	Left turn.
16.5	37.829632	107.157708	This is Highway 149 between mile posts 46 & 45. Turn right. Reset trip meter.
The Stony Pass road up the Rio Grande 3.6 miles to the right, between mile posts 42 & 41. The Silver Thread Campground is across the road. Lake City is left. Creede is right.			

NAVIGATION FOR DAY 3 CONTINUED

This table begins where the previous table left off on Highway 149 south of Silverton, Colorado. After connecting to Highway 149, turn right.

ODO	Latitude N	Longitude W	Landmarks and descriptions
The following odometer readings were taken using a '97 Isuzu Trooper. The GPS positions were acquired by referencing Google Maps.			
0.0	37.790078	107.129102	Between mile post 41 & 42, turn west on Rio Grande Road.
3.3	37.789338	107.180013	Left. Stay on 520. You will be on 520 all the way over Stony Pass to Howardsville.
8.4	37.738703	107.213669	Straight through is left. Stay on 520
12.6	37.724718	107.283996	There is an Outhouse at the lake.
17.4	37.769411	107.350580	Lost Trail Creek Campground. Fee required.
21.2	37.764447	107.397085	Brewster Park Cattleguard
22.2	37.749209	107.428536	Timber Hill. Right fork.
23.5	37.747867	107.431704	Bandit Rock.
25.1	37.751628	107.455648	Photo Rock. A beautiful place to park your car with a scenic background in the photo.
26.0	37.762159	107.466943	Stay to the right. Beartown is left. It's a three-hour round trip to Kite Lake.
32.2	37.795549	107.549235	This is Stony Pass. 12,590 feet.
34.7	37.816807	107.569676	Stay left. Right is Buffalo Boy Mine where the tram originates.
36.3	37.815392	107.578331	Intersection for San Juan County 3 and 4. Go across intersection staying on main road past Tramway House. This was Niegoldtown.
38.0	37.835680	107.595013	Howardsville. Elevation 9,640. Silverton is left. Eureka is right.

Note: The trail from Old Carson to Highway 149 is frequently muddy and slippery. It is best to travel this area with others. It is not heavily traveled so if you get into trouble, it can be a long walk out. Sections of that trail are rated Difficult.

Waterfalls are everywhere in the San Juan Mountains. They vary in size from very small to very tall.

BLACK BEAR ROAD

THE KING OF LEGENDS

When it comes to legends, this one is king of Colorado. It has appeared in every 4X4 magazine in existence and, like a famous gunslinger, its name is still whispered around 4-wheeler campfires from coast to coast. To conquer Black Bear is to out-fox Butch Cassidy, to beat Bat Masterson at poker, or to out-draw Kid Curry. To conquer Black Bear is to conquer a legend.

But what of the legend? Why is it a legend?

Black Bear is a one-way road. Like an outlaw on the run, it denies its own name. Although it appears as a road on the Forest Service Map, you won't find the name, "Black Bear" or any other name applied to it. The USGS county map includes the road but also refuses to name it. The closest it comes is a mark on the map for the Black Bear Mine. Just as there is no evidence Butch Cassidy died in a gun battle, there is no evidence that Black Bear Road exists ... but it is there.

It's the first road on the right, south of Red Mountain Pass on Route 550, between Silverton and Ouray. But where does the legend begin?

Overlooking Telluride

Ingram Falls

Getting to the highest point on the Black Bear Road is an easy task.

In fact, an experienced driver could get there in a two-wheel drive truck. At that point, the traveler is looking over Ingram Basin and down to the city of Telluride. But is that the point where the legend begins?

An argument can be made that four-wheel-drive (4WD) is required to begin the descent, but it is a weak argument. In fact, if the road is dry, the only critical part of the vehicle is the brakes. Texan once proved that theory when he lost his front differential and removed the front drive shaft. He finished the entire Black Bear Road with only the rear axle pulling.

From that highest point to the other side of Ingram basin, the road drops 1500 ft. in elevation. It snakes back and forth along the basin wall, passing the Black Bear Mine on the way, but does so gradually with no serious switchbacks or frightening turns. Slowly, but surely, the driver is sucked into lair of the legend. It's all so-o-o-o easy, so-o-o-o very easy, and then ... the legend begins!

I was there! I was in the infamous switchback before I knew it ... the one that has appeared in all the 4X4 magazines ... at least once. I was in the middle of it. It was so sharp ... and the turning area was so small. I eased the Bronco as far left as it would go, then cranked it so hard to the right, the power steering screamed for relief. Slowly ... so slowly, the Bronco began to turn ... but there just wasn't enough room! I knew I had to pull as far forward as possible to backup for another try.

I looked out the window on the driver's side and looked at the tire. There was still some distance to the edge. I eased off the brake ... only briefly ... the truck seemed to lunge forward ... like the strike of a snake ... from the pull of gravity. I slammed on the brake again and leaned back out the window.

The tires were on the edge of no return. Small pebbles rolled down from the edge of the cliff under the weight of the vehicle. There was no room for error! There was not an inch to spare!

I shoved the shift lever into reverse. But was it really in reverse? What if it was in forth gear? I was pushing on the clutch and brake so hard both legs were beginning to shake. Small beads of sweat began to break out on my forehead, and I could feel little beads rolling down my sides from my underarms.

Was this it? Was this the end of Pass Patrol's fearless leader and 4-wheeling fanatic. The silence inside the vehicle was deafening. No one was breathing.

Slowly ... very slowly ... my shaking leg began letting out on the clutch. I felt the engine pulling against the brake ... and it was going backwards. I let off the brake and breathed the first time in what seemed like hours. "Yeah!"

"We interrupt this program for a special announcement. He's lying."

"Who me? Lying?"

"Yeah, Outlaw. Your imagination is getting carried away. You are beginning to sound like a ten-cent magazine story."

"Okay. So that never happened. So, I have never had a tense moment on Black Bear. If I don't make it sound the way it sounds in the magazines, no one will read my story. Besides, there are people out there who will see Black Bear exactly as I described it."

"That's beside the point. You must tell the truth."

"But what about the legend. Saying Black Bear is a pussy cat is like saying Kid Curry was a wimp."

"The truth!"

Okay. Here's my real impression of Black Bear.

The trip across Ingram Basin is one of the most beautiful and scenic anywhere in the state, but not exactly challenging. At the edge of that basin is the vertical cliff where the Black Bear legend begins. It drops 2000 feet in elevation to the city of Telluride and it does so almost instantly.

The descent begins with some serious rock crawling along side Ingram Falls. That section is the most difficult section of the road. Extra care must be taken to keep from banging the underside of the vehicle. Lots of braking must be applied. The angle of descent is hair raising and the surface consists of going down a series of steps on loose gravel. No matter how slowly you go, the vehicle is going to slide on the rocks. Fortunately, it is a very short section of the road.

I once had a driver in the group that froze at that point. I walked back uphill to his truck and talked him down the steps. He made it with some coaching but the next option was to drive it down for him.

A Jeep rental company once told me they had a fellow that froze on the switchbacks. He just left the vehicle and walked back to the rental store with keys in hand. The point is that folks with a fear of heights, best stay off Black Bear Road.

At the bottom of that section is the first switchback which has been widened significantly during the past two years. In fact, several vehicles could now be parked side by side on the switchback. The road then becomes noticeably narrower as it passes beneath Ingram Falls and approaches the second switchback.

It is this second turn that is extremely frightening to some people.

There is no place to widen the road without dynamiting the mountain so it remains the most threatening turn on the road. It is the opinion of most everyone in our group that it is so obviously dangerous, it is not dangerous at all. Most of the time, when 4-wheelers get into trouble, it is because they were caught off guard. There is no way to be off guard at this switchback (unless you have already passed out from the first one). On the other hand, there have been folks that died on this trail by not knowing their own limitations.

There are several more potentially dangerous switchbacks ahead. Avoid the natural tendency to cut the switchbacks too soon.

Swing wide, then cut back. It will be necessary to make at least two attempts on many of them. The best approach is to have someone outside the vehicle watching the position of the tires. Pull forward as far as you safely can, put it in reverse, and back up. If you stop to take pictures, turn your wheels toward the bank, lock the emergency brake (never trust the "P" in an automatic to hold the vehicle), and turn off the engine.

We have given you two opposite versions of how you might view the descent on Black Bear Road. Both versions are potentially real. It's your turn.

It is 14 miles from Red Mountain Pass to Telluride using Black Bear Road. C.W. McCall wrote a song about his jeep going over the edge when his wife put a grapefruit-sized rock under the tire.

Black Bear Road ends at the bottom of Bridal Veil Falls.

The power house at the top is private property and is always being worked on by someone. Rumor has it that the current owners actually have it producing electricity. The area at the bottom of the falls is also posted as private.

Bridal Veil Falls Power Station is private property.

Most experienced 4-wheelers will consider Black Bear Road
to be an easy, but exhilarating, experience that must be repeated

many times. If you have a fear of heights, ride with someone else and follow the vehicle on foot through the sections that frighten you. You can also take one of the many tours from Ouray and let the guides do the driving. Whatever way you decide to do it, you and everyone who loves getting Rocky Mountain High, and loves to admire beautiful scenery, just must see the world from Black Bear Road.

GETTING LOST IN STYLE

The Uncompahgre National Forest Service Map has Black Bear Road on it and has marked it as One-Way-Only. The USGS county maps for San Juan County and San Miguel County are both needed to cover the whole trail.

BLACK BEAR ROAD NAVIGATION

Black Bear Road is easy to find … almost as easy as driving off a cliff. (Pun intended.)

Just go to Red Mountain Pass south of Ouray. Turn right on the first road south of the pass. At the first intersection, stay right. Beyond that point are more intersections but they all go to the same places.

ADDED NOTES

The following photo of Black Bear Road was taken from the Imogene Pass Road. From there, it is easy to see the number of switchbacks needed to descend the 1500 feet in elevation.

Black Bear Road view from the Imogene Pass Road

If heights frighten you, this is not a place you should go. You are only inches away from the edge of a cliff that drops more than 1,000 feet. One wrong turn and it's the pearly gates.

We rate it "Moderate and SCARY". The moderate part is almost an exaggeration. The surface is solid. Except for a few spots at the descent beside Ingram Falls, traction is good. The scary part of the rating applies to anyone with a fear of heights. Maybe we should add "Dangerous" to the rating. Several people have died on this road by going over the edge.

GOLIATH MEETS DUSTY

It was 1 a.m. in the morning on a cold Colorado night. The owner of a full-sized Blazer stood beside the trail shaking his head. Earlier in the day, his vehicle had slipped off the trail into a monstrous ditch that had instantly swallowed it all the way up to its bumpers. The tops of his 35-inch mudder-tires were barely peaking over the surface of the goo and when they turned, the vehicle did nothing more than stir the slop.

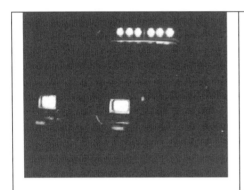 

Suddenly the night sky lit up in the distance and he heard the steady hum of two 4X4s. The lead vehicle was equipped with six Warn 100-watt off road lights that seemed to turn day into night. The driver pulled up alongside him. "Need a tug?"

He giggled while looking at the small Rocky and then back at his full-sized vehicle … complete with six-inch lift and 35-inch mudder tires. "That would be like David tugging on Goliath!"

"Hidden in the black bumper of this Rocky is a Warn XD9000 winch. If you want out, we'll get you out. Besides, the handle is Dusty … not David," Dusty said with a smile.

The Rocky backed up the trail and was anchored to the second vehicle with a tow strap. The winch cable was connected to the Blazer and the rest is history.

The Blazer owner walked back to the Rocky. "How much I owe you?"

"One 4-wheeler I.O.U." That meant the next time he met a 4-wheeler in trouble, he paid his debt by helping. "It's an unwritten 4-wheeler code," Dusty grinned. "And try to keep that thing on the trail. Warn and Pass Patrol believe it's important to Tread Lightly!"

KEEP THEM DOGGIES ROLLIN'

An experienced 4-wheeler protects his vehicle by making his tires take the abuse. When a big rock gets in the way, he runs a tire right over the top of it. When he has a step to climb, he backs the tires away from it a few inches and bumps it. The tires are aired down to 20 pounds so they will flex when they take the bump. It's an art that can't be described, but it can be taught. The bottom line is, the tires of a 4X4 take more abuse than any other part of the vehicle … on purpose.

Up until a few years ago, I was blowing an average of three tires a year. Then I noticed Caveman was running the same set for two years in a row, so I walked over to see what they were. That was my first real exposure to the B.F. Goodrich Radial All Terrain T/A. I haven't blown out a tire since, and the trails I've done during the past six years were not easy. I was so impressed, I contacted B.F. Goodrich and told them so. A short time later, B.F. Goodrich joined us as a product sponsor and soon after became members of Pass Patrol. That was in 1992.

So, what's the secret?

They were more than happy to show us a cutaway view of the tire. It has a three-ply sidewall. That's a feature I didn't know any radial tire had. But then, it doesn't matter to me anyway. All I care about is these tires don't give up when I need them the most.

And there is another benefit beyond durability. We noticed they don't hydroplane like our other tires did when we hit pockets of water on the Interstate Highway. And you won't believe how much better they get around in the snow.

I have become accustomed to having people I don't know thank me for recommending B.F. Goodrich Radial All Terrain T/A tires in my books and videos.

IMOGENE PASS – 13,114

2ND HIGHEST PASS ROAD IN THE USA

It is the shortest way to get back to Ouray from Telluride ... in miles that is. The trail takes you up a narrow shelf road on the opposite side of the valley from Black Bear. That means you get a really nice bird's eye view of the switchbacks and Bridal Veil Falls.

The 3500-foot climb from Telluride to the pass is fairly gradual except for the last few hundred feet, so depending on your gear ratio, you may be able to make the whole trip without ever engaging the front axle. The trail is narrow in places, but nothing like Black Bear.

Years ago, the road's primary purpose was to connect Telluride with the Savage Basin Camp. A daily stagecoach carried passengers and mail back and forth between the two cities.

Savage Basin had a school, a store, and a stable to serve the many miners who worked the Tomboy Mine starting about 1894.

The person who lived in the leaning cabin could not have known which way was up. Keeping coffee in the pot must have been a real challenge. I wonder if he had one short leg.

Most of Savage Basin Camp is gone now, but there are still a lot of foundations scattered around. Of course, most everything is posted as private. Apparently, at one time, the camp nearly filled the whole basin.

Imagine how harsh the weather must have been living above 12,000 feet. Cold winds and deep snow must have been routine nine months out of the year. What hardy breeds those people must have been to live in Savage Basin. Its name tells it all.

The trail meanders aimlessly through the ruins of Savage Basin, then makes an aggressive climb upwards to the pass. I have done this section in a full-size Bronco in two-wheel drive using the creeper gear, but the gears in my Rocky are not low enough requiring me to shift into low range.

In 1903, the State Militia constructed Fort Peabody on the top of Imogene Pass, 13,117-feet above sea level. Its purpose was to protect Telluride from (no, not Indians) striking miners.

The main issue at the time was to reduce the 12-hour work day to only 8 hours. The mine owners just would not hear of such foolishness. They brought in scab labor and, of course, the result was terminal for many on both sides.

When the miners threatened an assault from the east, the State Militia was assigned to shut down the pass. What an assignment. Take a look around.

Those poor guys were not exactly assigned to garden spot, USA. And the way voices carry in the mountains, they could probably hear the laughter of parties going on in Telluride.

The trail down goes pretty quick. It is another narrow shelf road that you should be getting used to. We don't rate Imogene too high in comparison to the others either in difficulty or in scenery,

It does have some really nice waterfalls. The photo below has one with a terrific photo op. It's a more enjoyable route to Ouray than taking the highway.

The last section of the trail has been constructed to route traffic around Camp Bird.

Some sections are rocky as in the photo above. Other sections are very muddy much of the time. Getting stuck in them would be extremely easy.

There are trails around the mud. If you decide to dip into one, better have someone waiting with a good winch. Those pockets have been known to swallow 4x4s up to the headlights.

GETTING LOST IN STYLE

The Uncompahgre National Forest map has the entire area on it.

IMOGENE PASS NAVIGATION

Imogene Pass Road - Telluride to Ouray
The main road through Telluride is W. Colorado Ave.

ODO	Latitude N	Longitude W	Landmarks and descriptions
The following odometer readings were taken using a '97 Isuzu Trooper. The GPS positions were acquired by referencing Google Maps.			
0.0	37.937939	107.813768	Turn right on N. Aspen St.
Go two blocks and turn right on E Galena Ave. Then go one block.			
0.0	37.939309	107.812105	Turn left on N. Oak St.
From a distance, N Oak Street looks more like a dead-end driveway for a house. The Imogene Pass Road turns to the right in front of that house.			
0.1	37.940113	107.811728	Follow the road to the right. It is the Tomboy Road and is closed in the winter.
4.6/0	37.938029	107.757044	This is Tomboy Basin where the mining took place.
A Historic sign marks the location. From the sign, the road goes through the old townsite and climbs the mountainside. Reset trip meter.			
1.8	37.931551	107.735210	Imogene Pass.
4.6	37.957306	107.723888	This is the area where the waterfall is located. Also, campsites.

6.4	37.975359	107.745319	Turn right on Yankee Boy Basin Road 26.
Right goes to Ouray. Left goes to Yankee Boy Basin.			

WILDERNESS DEFINED

"If a coyote howls in the night ... but no one is there to hear it ... does it make a sound?"

"If a bald eagle soars over the mountain's top and disappears into the shadows of a canyon ... but no one was there to see it ... was it really there?"

"If the most pleasant fragrance in the world comes from a flower found only in one location of the Colorado Rocky Mountains ... but no one is ever there to smell it ... is it just a myth?"

Every day of the week, SOMEONE in a prominent political position is doing everything he or she can, to make sure YOU never hear, see, or smell anything in much of Colorado's public lands ... and ... THEY SAY they are doing it for you!

THEY SAY Wilderness only includes roadless areas with no evidence of man's existence ... unscarred territory that is the same as it was two hundred years ago ... before man arrived. THEY SAY they are preserving it for you and your children.

Let's examine what THEY SAY. For example, the most recently passed Wilderness Bill in Colorado, closed the road up Oh-Be-Joyful Canyon. Within the area we are no longer allowed to visit, there is a road that has existed for more than one hundred years. It leads to an old cabin and an abandoned mining camp. That Wilderness Bill closed many miles of public access roads to some of the most scenic and historic lands in the state. Within those boundaries are century-old mining camps that flourished less than one-hundred years ago and are still visited regularly by those of us who love that country. So much for Wilderness including only roadless areas.

But, are they preserving it for us and our children? Once it is designated as wilderness (by the current government definition) neither you nor your children will ever see it again ... unless of course you can live out of a backpack for weeks at a time. The wildlife, the rivers, and the historic sites will become the private property of a small handful of people who can carry a sixty-pound backpack up and down 14,000-foot mountains and survive on dried trail foods for weeks at a time.

WILDERNESS DEFINED: No motorized vehicles allowed! Not even on existing roads!

The most vocalized argument for Wilderness is, "preserving it for future generations." If that is truly their purpose, they should have no objections to passing a newly revised Wilderness Definition stating that all vehicle roads and trails that now exist or have existed in the past two hundred years must be left open or reopened so this and future generations can enjoy the Wilderness.

"DON'T LET THEM LOCK YOU OUT!"

Write your senator today! Write to:

(Your senator's name),

UNITED STATES SENATE,

WASHINGTON DC 20510.

It's enough to make a lone wolf cry.

PASS PATROL'S SCHOOL OF HARD KNOCKS.

EXPLORING 101

Throughout history, there has always been the pioneer ... the wanderer ... THE EXPLORER. The one who rode his trusty steed into parts unknown, "In search of ... in search of ...."

No, he couldn't explain it. He may have claimed to be searching for better grazing land, but the true explorer never stayed. He left it to the ranchers and moved on.

He may have claimed to be searching for fertile farming land, but the true explorer never plowed it. He left it to the farmers and moved on.

He may have claimed to be searching for gold, but the true explorer never worked the claims he found. He sold it, usually for pennies, and upon his steed he faded into the horizon.

So, what was it the explorer was searching for? He took nothing from the land except what he needed to survive and he left nothing more than the tracks of his trusty steed to mark his passing. What was he looking for, indeed?

The explorer is still alive today. Oh, he's more modern all right ... and he's learned how to do his searching while enjoying the comforts of modern technology, but he is still searching. You'll find him in the most desolate places man can go. You'll find him in the most beautiful settings nature has to offer. You'll find him poking along a mountain trail, or meandering across the parched desert, or bouncing down a rocky hillside ... but if you look ... you'll definitely find him ... still searching

His trusty steed is a modern day 4X4 vehicle ... no not the monster trucks you see on TV ... the same 4X4 vehicles you see every day, going back and forth to work. He is the modern-day weekend pioneer ... the wanderer ... the explorer. Next time you see him, ask him what he's searching for, but be prepared for an answer that only another explorer will understand.

Or maybe no answer at all.

Happy Trails!

MEDANO PASS

9,649 Ft. elevation

The old saying is, "The more things change, the more things stay the same."

Medano Pass has changed. It used to be a mud-slingin', wheel-spinnin', slip pin' & slidin' bunch of fun. It is now a 4-wheeler's Sunday afternoon drive down a gravel road. The Forest Service has obviously expended a lot of money and sweat on this trail. "The more things change ...."

"... the more things stay the same." Medano Pass is the same. It has always been one of the most scenic and enjoyable drives for miles in any direction. The stream crossings are exciting in the spring and the sand at the end of the trail is a whole new experience for those of us who spend most of our time rock crawling.

Some will say the trail has been ruined ... others will say it has been improved. Some will say the environment is being protected ... others will say man has interfered by changing the course of the rivers. Our only comment is, "We miss the way it was ... we enjoy the way it is."

The miles of mud are gone, replaced by graded gravel-like surfaces. The stream bottoms are so solid, high clearance vehicles can wade through them without spinning a tire.

They can still be very deep during spring thaw so flooding an engine can still be your worst nightmare. With those new fuel injected systems, you can suck that cold water right into the cylinder and blow out the sides. Find out where your air intake is and be sure you won't get water in it. Then, "Go slow."

About half way down, you'll find the remains of what appears to be a ghost ranch.

The main house was still standing back in 1985, but some @-+*@ burned it down. The only buildings left could have been bunk houses for the hired hands, but no promises.

When you see the sand dunes for the first time, they look like mountains.

Maybe that's because they are. If you don't believe it, try climbing to the top of one. It is a lot of work.

The park service recommends that you lower your air pressure down to 15 pounds in all four tires. They have air pumps at the dunes campground for those who do not have their own.

We have never lowered our pressure just because we are too lazy to put it back in.

Since we travel in groups, we aren't too concerned about getting back out if we do get stuck. If you travel alone and get into something you can't get out of, the park service will be happy to assist for several hundred dollars.

Driving in the sand is like learning to drive all over again, especially if you keep your tire pressure up. The most interesting sections of the trail are the ones going uphill. You must select the right gear so you can keep moving without bogging down the engine. There are plenty of side trails where you can practice hill climbs. Be sure to stay on the existing trails.

Most of the dunes are restricted to hiking. Be sure to take plenty of water and a compass. Once you get between the hills in the dunes, it is nearly impossible to tell which way is back. The wind always blows and will cover your footprints in minutes.

A video at the visitor center is very helpful in understanding how these 1000-foot-high mountains of sand came into existence. The kids will love rolling down the sides of the dunes and die-hard skiers will enjoy new-found slopes. There are no ski lifts though, so be prepared to earn your thrills.

MEDANO PASS NAVIGATION

From Westcliffe, Colorado, take Highway 69 south for 23.2 miles. The trail to Medano Pass is just past mile post 35. It is marked with a forest service sign calling it FSR 559.

The following odometer readings were taken using a '97 Isuzu Trooper. The GPS positions were acquired by referencing Google Maps.			
ODO	Latitude N	Longitude W	Landmarks and descriptions
23.2	37.836468	105.307557	Go west on FSR 559.

You will climb for miles in a westerly direction to the summit of Medano Pass.

The following odometer readings were taken using a '97 Isuzu Trooper. The GPS positions were acquired by referencing Google Maps.			
ODO	Latitude N	Longitude W	Landmarks and descriptions
41.1	37.855784	105.432149	Medano Pass.

There is a gate and fence at that point with a road going off to the right. That road to the right goes toward Medano Lake but you'll have to hike if you want to reach the lake. It may have been closed by the last Wilderness Bill.

The road going through the gate goes to the dunes. There are several camping areas on both sides of the pass and the park service has a campground with all the luxuries down at the dunes.

MAP FOR MEDANO PASS

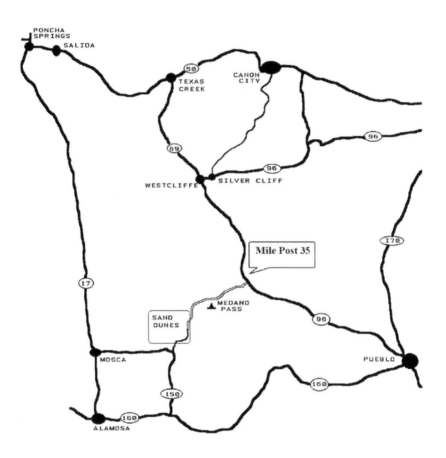

GETTING LOST IN STYLE

The Rio Grande National Forest Map covers the area.

PASS PATROL'S SCHOOL OF HARD KNOCKS

ROCK CRAWLING 101

You will be amazed at what your good ole stock 4X4 will go over and what it will go through without suffering permanent damage, but it does take skill. Mostly, it takes patience. In many of our tales, you will notice we are driving slower than we could be walking. But then, if we wanted to hurry, we could have spent the day dodging cars on I-25 through Denver.

Our School of Hard Knocks is our way of telling you how we avoid getting knocks from rocks and other things that go bump in the night ... or day! Ouch!

When rock crawling, you do just the opposite of what you would do driving down I-25. If you see something in the road on I-25, you straddle it or swerve around it. Most trails are not wide enough to go around anything and you cannot drive off the trail. If you straddle a big rock, you will probably bang the underside of your vehicle. The solution is to aim a tire directly at it. As the tire goes over the biggest rock, it raises the rest of the vehicle safely above all the other rocks.

Some day when you're not real busy, lay down in front of your vehicle and look under it. Note your lowest points. Learn to tell where those points are while sitting in the driver's seat. There are times when you just can't avoid straddling a rock. If you know where your highest clearance point is, you can position the vehicle to go over it with the best chance of clearing the object. If you still can't clear the object, move some rocks in front of your tires so you can clear the vehicle as you drive over the rocks.

If you have a narrow base vehicle and you can go between the big stuff, then do it. No sense in getting one side way up and the other down. You might scare the kids.

Remember, the most abused part of your vehicle should be your tires. Use them to protect everything else.

PASS PATROL'S SCHOOL OF HARD KNOCKS

GETTING LOST IN STYLE

Never let'um see ya sweat! When you get lost, just pull over to the side of the road and spread a topo map out across the hood. When someone comes by and asks if you are lost, say, "Naw! I'm just studying the land formations and lining them up on the map." If they notice you have the map upside down, just say, "Yeah. I'm testing myself to see if I come up with the same elevation points while turning the map in various directions."

They will go away shaking their heads, but that's okay. They can't prove anything. Wait until they get a short distance away, then load up the truck and follow them out.

One small caution: Be sure you follow someone who is going out ... not in.

If you would like to have some topo maps, USGS will be happy to sell you all you can carry. The best ones for Colorado are the county series. For Utah, the best ones are the 1:100,000. If you need real serious detail, the 7.5 minute maps have it but to cover a small area will cost enough to eat up your next car payment in a heartbeat. To find your local USGS map sales in the phone book, look under **Government listings**, then look under "**Interior– Dept. of**", then under "**Geological Survey**", then look for "**Map Sales**".

The US Forest Service maps are cheaper and cover a larger area, but they are not as detailed. To find your local USFS map sales in the phone book, look under **Government listings**, then look under "**Agriculture– Dept. of**", then under "**Forest Service**".

If you don't have a local office for either one, look in the yellow pages under, "Maps" for dealers.

Pass Patrol is never lost. We call it "Exploring." We do a lot of "Exploring." In fact, Trapdoor and Outlaw were recently exploring for two days before they found another town.

Happy Trails!

PASS PATROL'S SCHOOL OF HARD KNOCKS

SURVIVAL 101

Selecting the food supply and keeping it from spoiling on a long trip is of major importance. Especially if you do not intend to be anywhere to get more supplies along the way. We have a simple technique that works great.

The first step is to get a decent quality cooler. Be sure the lid seals tightly when closed. The cooler should be tall enough that a two-liter soft drink bottle will stand straight up. It must be roomy inside to hold everything mentioned on this page.

Don't put anything in the cooler that won't spoil or does not need to be cold. Leave that space for ice and food that spoil. For example, you may have several bottles of your favorite drink but you only drink one at a time so only put one bottle in at a time. Meat items should be put into sealable bags. The bags should be placed into a sealable container. The container I use is large enough to stand up in the center of the cooler and holds all my sealable bags for a seven-day supply. For a family of four, you will probably need more than one cooler for a week-long trip.

Get the two-liter bottles used for soft drinks. Fill them with water and freeze them solid. The size of the cooler and the length of the trip will determine how many you need. Place them in the outside corners of the cooler. Put the food container in the center. Pack the rest of the cooler with chunk/cube ice. Avoid crushed ice because it melts quicker. Put the ice chest inside the vehicle and cover it with a blanket or sleeping bag. Using this method, I have still had crushed ice at the end of a week and the bottle ice will often last even longer. As the bottles thaw, they become your drinking water.

The choice of foods for the trip should be based on what you like to eat. Some of our members prepare food ahead of time, put it in self-sealing plastic bags, and freeze it. For example, they can prepare a beef stew dinner by simply placing the bag in boiling water for a few minutes. I prefer easy to cook items such as steaks, pork chops, bacon, eggs and lunch meats.

Always carry a good supply of canned goods such as ready to eat soups and stews. I normally plan for a can of soup every evening to reduce the amount of spoilable food to carry. Keep plenty of canned goods around as emergency rations. I carry enough emergency rations to last a week longer than I plan to stay.

Be sure you have plenty of batteries for the flash lights and don't forget the matches. Fire starter can be handy if you are expecting damp weather. Be sure you have plenty of water, especially in the desert. A first aid kit should be handy and every vehicle should have a tow strap.

Carry at least one hydraulic jack. Bumper jacks raise the vehicle too high so you need one that will go under the axle.

In one quick summary, "Be prepared."

THE END

Black Bear Road

Pass Patrol Recollections

VOLUME ONE

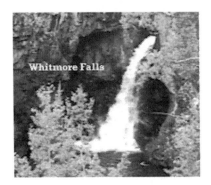

Whitmore Falls

Haggerman Pass

Imogene Pass Road near Savage Basin

LONE WRITER TALES and TRAILS

World Wide on the Web at www.Lone-Writer.com

Made in United States
Troutdale, OR
06/17/2025

32187244R00106